Huey Morgan's Rebel Heroes

Dedicated to my mother,
who taught me to ask why.

Huey Morgan's Rebel Heroes

THE RENEGADES OF MUSIC & WHY WE STILL NEED THEM

Huey Morgan

CASSELL ILLUSTRATED

An Hachette UK Company
www.hachette.co.uk

First published in Great Britain in 2015 by Cassell Illustrated, a division of
Octopus Publishing Group Ltd
Carmelite House
50 Victoria Embankment
London EC4Y 0DZ
www.octopusbooks.co.uk

Commissioning Editor: Hannah Knowles
Editor: Pauline Bache
Creative Director: Jonathan Christie
Senior Production Manager: Peter Hunt

ISBN (hardback) 978 1 84403 837 4
ISBN (paperback) 978 1 84403 875 6

A CIP catalogue record for this book is available from the British Library.

Printed and bound in the UK

13 5 7 9 10 8 6 4 2

CONTENTS

INTRODUCTION: LONG LIVED ROCK'N'ROLL

Rock 'n' Roll died with a bang on 5 April 1994, when Kurt Cobain blew his head off. It took them three days to discover his body, but when they did, that was the end of Rock 'n' Roll as we knew it. As I knew it.

Kurt once said, 'I'd rather be hated for who I am than loved for who I am not.' He looked into that Warholian crystal ball and realized that in the future he would no longer be recognized for his music or his words or his thoughts. He realized that he was going to be famous in the way that someone like Kim Kardashian is famous: for who he was fucking, or fighting, or friends with. He would be famous for what he did, who he did it with and when he did it. The things of worth he had achieved as an icon of grunge – as an anti-establishment, anti-hero, singular figure who stood up for the other geeks, nerds and misfits – would merit scant screen space in a media driven by salacious gossip and inane opinion.

You can't revere both Kurt Cobain and Kim Kardashian. You have to pick a side, and Kurt picked his side with a shotgun in his mouth. Kurt saw the future and thought, 'Fuck this, I'm out.'

I got into making music with the Criminals around 1994, and I could feel the end was coming; everything was running out of steam. The real Rock 'n' Rollers were sprinting with a dying Olympic torch that was steadily being extinguished by outmoded record labels and capitalist companies seeking 'brand alignment' with the day's hottest musicians. Pre-Nineties, musicians made music because they needed to; they had a hole to fill, a desire to make something that no one had heard before. They had something to say and we, the people, wanted – and needed – to hear it.

You can pretty much pinpoint 1993–96 as the beginning of the end: the White House launching its first web page; the introduction of animal cloning; the first genetically engineered tomato hit the market; O J Simpson running wild in his Bronco, live on TV, while everyone's at home on dial-up to see John Wayne Bobbitt get his schlong cut off. The writing was on the wall and it spelled 'Rock 'n' Roll Is Dead. Long Lived Rock 'n' Roll'.

In the midst of all that, one of music's most seminal figures decided to check out. Kurt's suicide symbolized the death of the rebellious spirit – and with it, a sense of individual identity and inherent creativity. Suddenly, the Internet and rolling news channels and an overwhelming access to information destroyed our attention spans. We stopped searching and we started accepting. There's no message in so much of the music being put out any more, except 'Buy me'. It's a side dish to whatever else you're doing, not the main meal. We know that music is devoid of soul because it exists only as background sound while we're doing something else. In the gym. At work. Entertaining friends at home. Music doesn't weigh enough. My Uzi doesn't weigh a ton any more – it weighs six ounces. And no one's trying to challenge that. The spirit of Rock 'n' Roll is that you don't give up. Ever. But that spirit died with Kurt.

Around the time Kurt took his life in the Nineties, everything stopped being fun and new and crazy. All the M25 raves were shut down and rave culture in the UK died. Hip-Hop turned into professional wrestling. House music would become bastardized by EDM, a multi-million-dollar record-label-branded industry rather than a genre trying to push the boundaries of dance music.

Everybody just gave up and went along with it.

Don McLean might have thought the music died the day Buddy Holly's plane came down in Iowa. And, sure, we lost a great Rock 'n' Roller with Holly. But for me, the definition of the Rock star – regardless of what genre he or she came from – died with Kurt. I think it's a damn shame and I think it's a damn shame we lost him. In the Nineties, records were being sold at an unbelievable rate and the amount of money being made was insane. Kurt wasn't prepared for the amount of cash he was raking in. This was a kid from Dirtsville, USA, who didn't have shit to his name. Couple that with his – by all accounts – fucked-up marriage, a history of depression and the realization that it was all a sham, and it's no wonder he popped his head off. And when he did, he burst the bubble. After that, everybody knew. Kurt knew he couldn't do what was expected of him any more. He couldn't be a parent and a husband *and* this version of a Rock star projected to the world via satellite radio and 24-hour news shows and Google Alerts. Kurt wouldn't want millions of followers on Twitter and Instagram or to talk about what he'd had for fucking breakfast.

After two World Wars and the Great Depression, people needed an escape. They'd struggled in the doom and gloom for long enough. That's when music started soothing ravaged souls on a national level in America – and on an international level too. Music became our artistic antidote to the cold, cold world. Music could help you figure out your problems – or forget them. It created like-minded tribes of people who would gather together in dark and dusty record shops, flicking tirelessly through miles of vinyl to find that rare seven-inch of James Brown's 'It's Hell'. It united us on dance floors and in dancehalls. It's what we fell in and out of love to, consoled ourselves about our shitty jobs with, or celebrated the births of our kids to. Music was the constant waypoint for both the significant and insignificant moments in our lives.

But I've become increasingly disillusioned over the last 20 years. As a huge fan of music – at points in my life you could almost call it an obsession – it breaks my heart to see the direction it's taken. Music has become, in many ways, a metaphor for our times. Now all we have is data; not knowledge, just data. We 'know' but we rarely experience or feel.

Nowadays labels and a lot of radio stations play, hire and buy what they know we will play, hire and buy. It's a marketing tool that's been perfected over the course of popular music's history. How are you going to sell music if you can't sell somebody some*thing*? So if it's not a CD you're buying, then it's a T-shirt or a perfume or a sneaker. I always equated the music industry with the drug game, but in the drug business, if you fuck up, you get killed. In the record industry, if you fuck up, you get a promotion – or, if you get fired, a healthy severance package and the chance to run another record company into the ground.

I have no illusions that writing this book will relight the flame of Rock 'n' Roll, but I hope like-minded individuals out there will be inspired to go and seek out the lost greats of our time. I hope more kids will go pick up the guitar or the drums or the pen and go and gig for the sheer love of it, rather than simply striving to become a celebrity of sorts. Our obsession with wealth and a misguided notion of fame has led us to desire an idea of success that simply doesn't exist and is neither satisfying nor sustaining.

I love music and I think – I hope – that comes through to the listener in the music I make and my radio shows. There's still some awesome music being made, but the spirit has been suffocated. It's time to let it breathe again.

STILL
GOT THE
BLUES

The Blues moves in truly mysterious ways. It was in Rock 'n' Roll, it was in Punk, it's in Hip-Hop – guys like Joe Strummer and Melle Mel were talking about politics and social issues just like the Blues men and women before them did. Even the term Rock 'n' Roll was first used by an old Blues singer called Trixie Smith, who had a song called 'My Man Rocks Me (With One Steady Roll)', in 1922; it was a euphemism for having sex – 'I wanna Rock 'n' Roll witchu, girl' – which pretty much sums it up. It's an old expression from back in the day that was co-opted into this all-encompassing definition that we use now in modern times.

Though times were incredibly tough at the turn of the twentieth century, it was a more permissible life in a lot of ways. In the days of the Blues, most substances were either legal – gin, cocaine, pot – or overlooked. Cocaine was big in the Blues era, more so than in later decades, because it was available over the counter. It's said to have been in Coca-Cola (the company strongly denies this). You could ask for it in the pharmacy and they'd say, 'Sure – liquid or powder?' 'Oh, I don't know. One of each!' It would get these guys up, get them going and get them jazzed up for the show that night. Or two shows that night. They'd be playing into the early hours, but it was no problem because they had coke to keep them going. With Jazz musicians, they had jazz cigarettes and they would get high before the show out back. They were having a fucking good time back then. The liberties that were afforded, especially to the minorities – at that point – were unprecedented if you were a musician. If you weren't a musician, you were kept in that segregated box far into the Sixties. Back then, if you were famous, rich or powerful, and you knew someone who worked in a pharmacy, you could order a pound of pharmaceutical cocaine. And you'd have a big old jar on your table ten minutes later. (In the Eighties, with the Hair bands, it got worse. If you didn't have whisky and coke in your system, you weren't in a band.)

Cocaine and weed were outlawed at slightly different times, but for pretty much the same reason – white women and the impotent rage of the white man. Drugs were seen as the gateway to white women hooking up with black men – and the white man didn't like that. At all. Coke was the first to be made illegal in 1914 and then pot went too in the mid-Thirties, when too many Jazz musicians in New Orleans – according to a white politician called Harry Anslinger – were trying to get with the white women. These guys, like the 'coke fiends' before them, were supposedly smoking pot and encouraging white women to smoke it too, and then they'd engage in wild, passionate sex. It was all based in religion: the white man wanted to keep his race 'clean'. Anslinger targeted that fear by appealing to the Ku Klux Klan and all those wackos by using overt racism to ban pot. He got people fired up by saying things like 'Their Satanic music, jazz and swing result from marijuana use. This marijuana causes white women to seek sexual relations with Negroes, entertainers and others.' Another one was 'Reefer makes darkies think they're as good as white men.' Pretty staggering, right? Considering this was less than a hundred years ago. So they made marijuana illegal. Anslinger screwed it up for everyone else.

But before then, the Blues men and women got away with a lot, because they were keeping the masses entertained, keeping everyone contained. No one was checking that part of the world too much. There were two Americas in the early part of the last century: Black America and White America. And no one cared about Black America apart from black Americans and maybe musicologist John Lomax. Lomax and his son, Alan Lomax, discovered Huddie 'Lead Belly' Ledbetter, who was in jail after being accused of murder, and persuaded the warden to pardon him on the basis of his talent. Not that White America was pleased. When the *New York Herald Tribune* reported on Lead Belly, it wrote: 'Sweet singer of the swamplands here to do a few tunes between homicides.' Still worse, *LIFE* magazine ran an article headed 'Bad Nigger Makes Good Minstrel.' The world was so different then. The rules were completely different for black folk than for white folk.

Back then, 'black music' and 'white music' were so separate that you could dip into black music and steal from it – like Elvis did – and no one in the mass white audience would be any the wiser. There's the obvious segregation that we know about – separate bathrooms, different sections of the bus – but the music was also totally segregated. There was the 'chitlin' circuit', where all the musicians who played were black. Then there was the 'regular circuit', where all the white musicians played, in dancehalls and the like. And then there was the higher end: the Cotton Club and the Apollo Theater, where all the top black musicians in New York would play. There were some white people going to those places. Every once in a while someone might be asked to play a private party downtown, or in someone's private house. But ultimately, there was total separation between Bill Haley & His Comets and B B King, for example. Artists could blatantly rip off black musicians and take that music and make it huge in the white charts.

In those times, people pretty much stayed within their own race. It was very segregated. Luckily, because of the Civil Rights Movement during the Sixties, more people started to understand about the different ways other people lived, and to care about them.

Without America being so fucked up, we might never have had this incredible music: the Blues, Jazz, Rock 'n' Roll and Hip-Hop. Adversity brings out the best and worst in people – but the best is what we're talking about now. The adversity that the black race, the African-American people faced in America was what made the music so real and so undeniably authentic. And people always want what's real.

The Blues started in the South and spread north as Southern folk fled to the city to escape financial hardships and the Jim Crow mentality. T Bone Burnett told me one time in an interview that 'the Mississippi is responsible for all popular music.' Its tributaries take it from New Orleans all the way to Chicago, and so all of these Blues musicians would hop on and off the boats, spreading the sound as they went. As the musicians moved north to cities like Detroit and Chicago, the sound metamorphosed from Country Blues to City Blues, later on becoming amplified by the likes of Howlin' Wolf, T-Bone Walker and B B King – who would sow the seeds for Hendrix, the Stones and Clapton.

When it came to music, what we call the Blues started through adversity. Through hatred, really. From being segregated and being treated like an animal. Knowing inside that you're as smart as, if not even smarter than, that guy. But because he's white, he's got a job that you can do better than he can.

The Blues was born out of wanting and needing to tell a story, to spread the notions of pain and poverty and love and hate to your fellow brothaman. Nowadays, music doesn't appear to be about guys or women actually telling a story, singing a song, playing a song, or writing a song and transmitting an emotion to someone else. That's been sacrificed for visual pleasure over aural experience. Because God knows who writes the songs for half these musicians nowadays.

*

THE DEVIL TAKE YOUR SOUL

There's a deep sense of spirituality to be found in the Blues, and not just because it emerged from the churches of the South. It's no wonder that people were looking to a higher power to save their souls back then; what other hope did you have? In the Southern black communities in the 1800s, music and religion were inextricably entwined. The 'Negro Spirituals' were about praising the higher power and creating a sense of community against the continuing slavery, unconcealed racism and entrenched poverty. The Spirituals and the Blues both conveyed the feeling of hopelessness and despair, but here they divided. Where the Spirituals were religious, the Blues were worldly. The Spirituals focused on a collective feeling, the Blues on the individual. There was often a sense of humour and optimism in the Blues too. 'My woman might have left me and I lost my job, but tomorrow I'm gonna get me a new woman! And maybe a new job!'

But it was a big deal for a lot of the Blues artists to swap church music for secular. And not just at the turn of the century – Aretha Franklin, for example, was a staunch churchgoer. The Faustian idea of selling your soul to the devil has been around for centuries, but it began in popular music with the legendary Robert Johnson. Johnson was a guitar player like no other; this man could really, really play the Blues. Eric Clapton declared Johnson to be 'the most important Blues musician who ever lived', while Keith Richards asked the question: 'Want to know how good the Blues can get? Well, this is it.' Johnson is the foundation of the Mississippi Blues and the foundation of Rock 'n' Roll. We only have 29 recordings that Johnson made around 1936–37 but their impact is still felt today: 'Cross Road Blues', 'I Believe I'll Dust My Broom', 'Terraplane Blues', 'Sweet Home Chicago', 'Love In Vain' and 'Hellhound on My Trail' proved Johnson to be one of the most original, distinctive voices in music. He sang with such pathos, with such pain, said Clapton, that it was as if 'he felt things so acutely that he found it almost unbearable'.

There are scant details about Johnson's short life. The illegitimate son of a sharecropper, he was born in Mississippi in 1911. He had grown up, typically for a black guy of that time, poor. He was relatively well educated; he attended school; he married his first wife at 18, though he was said to be a womanizer. He played guitar and harmonica and sang, and worked his way around the juke joints and street corners of the South, getting himself a little reputation. A contemporary of his, Son House, remembered him to be a competent harmonica player but a dreadful guitarist. Around 1929, Johnson disappeared. No one saw or heard from him for weeks. Apparently he had taken his guitar to the crossroads of Highways 49 and 61 in Clarksdale, Mississippi. There, legend has it, he met with the devil, who, in exchange for his soul, bestowed upon Johnson complete mastery of the guitar. On his return from the crossroads, his proficiency was remarkable, and so began the spread of the Faustian myth surrounding him. Johnson did little to discourage this, often alluding to the fact he'd struck a deal with Satan. When he died at the age of 27 – poisoned by the jealous husband of a woman he'd been hitting on – he became the inaugural member of the infamous '27 Club', only adding to the illusion of mystery and dark powers at work. The crossroads pact became as big a part of Johnson's myth as the music.

As I said, religion, particularly at that point, was ingrained in society; it was a big fucking deal back then in the American South. To say you were side-by-side with the devil was unthinkable in the eyes of a pious person. Did Johnson really sell his soul? I imagine he holed himself up for a couple of months and practised like a motherfucker – you do anything enough you're gonna get good at it. Or he got himself into some drugs and let his mind and his fingers wander. He made up the devil story so everyone left him alone. And it made for a better story too!

Johnson is so key in the history and development of music because he created the idea of the modern Blues man, the archetypical Blues man; he had the hat and the suit and the slide guitar and he's talking about the devil and women and whisky and the torture of being a lonely, wandering soul. Whatever happened that meant Johnson was able to play the guitar like he played it, I don't care. Because of it, we got some of the best Blues ever created, while the seeds for Rock 'n' Roll were sown at the same time.

*

SPREADING THE GOSPEL

The Blues came to me through a childhood friend of mine, Peter, who's since passed away. He lived in the building next to mine on New York's Lower East Side, where I grew up. He was a little older than me. He had diabetes and was later confined to a wheelchair so he didn't get around much but he'd make it to the bench where we'd be hanging out. He played guitar and we'd talk to him about stuff and eventually he taught me how to get into playing guitar. Like, really *playing* the guitar. He played me a live recording by Albert King and I was blown away. It was from 1969 at the Fillmore East in New York, when King was opening up for Jimi Hendrix on New Year's Eve. You hear King after the first song, bewildered, saying 'Thank you' as all these white kids go crackers. He was a huge influence on the likes of Hendrix, Stevie Ray Vaughan and Clapton. King was known as one of the 'Three Kings of Blues Guitar', alongside B B King and Freddie King. He'd grown up picking cotton in the fields of Mississippi in the Thirties, before getting into guitar as a teen. He was around in the Fifties, but became a lot more popular in the Sixties, like a lot of the older Blues musicians who were being referenced by the likes of Hendrix and Keith Richards. I'd heard Led Zeppelin records before then, but as soon as Peter played me Albert King I was like, 'Oh, *that's* where that comes from.' So much of what we listen to as music derives from the Blues and therefore black culture. For instance, Led Zeppelin: that's black music. Even when it gets down to New Yorkers playing Folk music, like Simon and Garfunkel, that was modern-day New York Blues. They were talking about 'Oh, Cecilia, you're breaking my heart... I'm down on my knees, I'm begging you please' and 'Bridge Over Troubled Water' and 'Homeward Bound'; all these tracks are Blues songs put in a different frame.

The Blues was also a means of communication between communities. A lot of conversation would be disguised in the music that black folk didn't want the white folk to hear. And, via the Mississippi's tributaries, it meant the conversation could be passed from Alabama to Chicago, in the same way that Hip-Hop would later tell Harlem what was happening in the Bronx. The Blues is a gloriously stealthy beast; it continues to pop up where you least expect it.

Then there was Elvis, who totally appropriated black culture but never particularly acknowledged the roots of what he was doing. That's not to say people didn't – or don't – pay homage. Keith Richards is a man who could happily kick back and think about all he's done with his life, but he talks endlessly about being a student of the Blues.

A master of the guitar for over 50 years insists he's still learning. I think that's pretty cool.

So, you see, everything is connected to the Blues; everything is connected to those roots. The Blues helped the shoots grow and it tended them, encouraging them to bend in different ways. There's nothing stopping the shoots reaching up to the skies; there's a good foundation and no ceiling. The tree's growth has the potential to be limitless; but unfortunately it's having sustenance problems right now.

BORN TO BE WILD (WOMEN)

If the spirit of Rock 'n' Roll died with Kurt Cobain, then Ma Rainey gave birth to that spirit. It was a woman – not a man – who delivered the Blues unto us.

Rainey, the woman known as the Mother of the Blues, is recognized as being both the first professional Blues performer and the person who really drove the recording explosion during the Twenties. There were other male recording artists of significance, of course – notably Memphis's W C Handy, aka the Father of the Blues, who composed a lot of the early standards, and Robert Johnson, who came along later, in the Thirties. Another key female figure, Mamie Smith, was the first black person to feature on a commercially recorded song, 'Crazy Blues', in August 1920. (Mamie took the place of the song's intended vocalist, a white Broadway singer named Sophie Tucker, who had fallen ill at the time of recording.) When white-owned labels like Paramount saw how fast 'n' furious 'Crazy Blues' and other so-called 'race records' were selling to black folk, they quickly realized the need to ignore the otherwise explicit racism that was the cornerstone of early-20th-century America. 'Crazy Blues' went on to sell over half a million copies, and all of a sudden black female vocalists were in demand. And none were more in demand than the magnificent Ma Rainey.

Rainey's musical life started when she was just a teen at the turn of the 20th century, touring the South with her then husband, 'Pa' Rainey, in the all-black travelling troupe the Rabbit Foot Minstrels. They later became known as the Assassinators of the Blues. Ma and Pa didn't last, and Rainey went solo; from 1923 onwards, she released over a hundred Blues recordings, some of which she'd written herself.

By the mid-1920s, the woman born Gertrude Pridgett in Georgia was a fully-fledged recording star being paid around $2,000 a week. Think about that: a black woman being paid $2,000 a week, in the Twenties. Before then, it had been tough for black and white women to work in any profession, with female entertainers regarded as little more than prostitutes. But with the advent of Rainey and the recording industry, slowly it became acceptable for women to make as much of a song and dance as their male counterparts.

Long before B-Boys in the Bronx were bouncing chains off their chests, Rainey was touring the country with a mouthful of gold teeth and a big-ass chain decorated with $20 gold pieces. Rainey was a major-league player, covering herself in gems, fancy headbands, feathers and furs. As her one-time manager, Thomas A Dorsey, said, 'When she started singing, the gold in her teeth would sparkle. She was in the spotlight. She possessed listeners; they swayed, they rocked, they moaned and groaned, as they felt the Blues with her.'

Rainey toured the country in an old tour bus with her band, including female pianist Lovie Austin, and – later on – the likes of Jazz legend Louis Armstrong. She would arrive on stage through a giant replica gramophone – the woman knew how to put on a show. She sang about promiscuity and heartbreak, about working hard and playing hard, and occasionally – as in 1928's 'Prove It On Me' – she alluded to her rumoured lesbianism: 'I went out last night with a crowd of my friends, It must have been women, 'cos I don't like no men', and 'It's true I wear a collar and a tie... Talk to the gals just like any old man.' Radical stuff for the Twenties – especially considering the frenzy caused by Katy Perry singing the fairly benign 'I Kissed a Girl' in the late Noughties.

The late, great Bessie Smith – aka the Empress of the Blues – was also known for her outrageous fashion and lavish parties. Like Rainey, Smith revelled in her sexuality with a sense of unadulterated pleasure. Check the track 'He's Got Me Goin'' as an example. Or this lyric from 1928's 'Empty Bed Blues': 'When he got to teachin' me, from my elbow down was sore.' Smith would also covertly nod to her bisexuality: 'When you see two women walking hand in hand, just look 'em over and try to understand. They'll go to these parties, have the lights down low, only those parties where women can go.' Back then, the Blues was infused with sexual imagery, relayed mostly through euphemism or via food metaphors – 'Anybody Here Want to Try My Cabbage' was the question posed by Maggie Jones! A lot of the times too, singers hid political messages within those same lyrics – if you knew what they were saying, then you knew what they was saying – something we would see replicated later on in the very early days of Hip-Hop. Via localized vernacular indecipherable to the casual listener (or more importantly, a judge!) the Bronx would communicate to Harlem who was running the streets, in the same way someone in Tennessee could describe their conditions to someone in Texas, back in the day.

Blues women were making so much money that they could do whatever they wanted. In terms of the respect they were afforded, Ma Rainey, Bessie Smith, Ethel Waters, Mamie Smith and other women were getting treated as good as the men – and financially they were treated even better. Bessie Smith was paid anywhere between $115 and $200 for a record. Her male counterpart on Columbia Records would receive as little as $15. These women were singing beautiful music and people were lapping it up, proving that money talks, bullshit walks.

Ma Rainey was known for being crazy and wild, but she was cool about it. And man, did she live the life. Rainey and Bessie Smith were the original wild women of music; gambling, drinking and drug use were par for the course for those two. Hellraisers like Rainey and Smith were as famous as the Rihannas and Beyoncés of today but with one key difference: no camera phones, no relentlessly invasive media. These women could do whatever the hell they wanted, and boy did they. You didn't have cameras in elevators back then, did you?

*

ANYTHING MEN CAN DO

Sex and drugs and Rock 'n' Roll wasn't invented by Hendrix, Jagger or Richards. Since the dawn of mankind, people have liked to have a good time, and the women of Blues were no different. Rainey and Smith were said to go to 'donkey shows', which was a euphemism for sex shows where the gentleman concerned would be very well endowed. They would go with him afterwards and they'd be smoking, drinking, shooting up, whatever – having fun with it, having sex with the guy. Because these women had so much clout, no one ever said anything; it wasn't a big thing like it is now.

Throughout music's history, women Rocked 'n' Rolled as hard as men, but it's largely ignored. Look at what the Go-Go's did back in the day; that was some pretty nasty stuff. They were incredibly Rock 'n' Roll. There was a video that surfaced of Belinda Carlisle and Kathy Valentine disrespecting their roadie so bad, making him jack off and putting vibrators up his ass. It was the unlawful, crazy-ass behaviour that you'd associate more with all-male bands, some of which were very, very sexually active with their fans. But that happened before the days of the Internet. Now, with camera phones around, the minute you misbehave, it's out there.

One reason that the women in Blues were popular was because they were 'allowed' to be. Bessie Smith and Ma Rainey were non-threatening to white audiences, because they weren't men. They weren't black men trying to 'take the white woman'. Black men were seen as threatening because the white man was scared that black men were going to inseminate the population. Women didn't pose quite the same threat, so there was no glass ceiling in popular music for black women back then.

Back then, the success was mostly local but immediate; we didn't have the global domination of a Miley Cyrus. But if you did good in your home state, you could buy a house. The Blues women were getting paid thousands; they were set and they were going nuts. They were young women and there were a lot of young men around. And good-looking ones too. Imagine Van Halen's dressing room in reverse. You'd have all these hot young boys in there with them, everyone smoking marijuana and drinking hooch. Everyone did what they wanted to do back then.

*

AN UGLY TRUTH

Women in music, far more than men, have been judged on their looks. Ma Rainey, for example, was known as being 'the ugliest woman in show business'. People judged, and continue to judge, women more on their looks than on their talent or abilities or intelligence. It's an incredibly sexist world we live in where it's still acceptable to say that a woman's unattractive, and judge her on that, when a man's looks are rarely called to attention in the same way. Luckily, some things transcend; Ma Rainey would sing and people would be blown away. The fact she wasn't what was considered classically beautiful would fade away in the face of her formidable talent.

Bobbie Gentry was another woman who refused to be a product, in the way that a lot of these earlier musicians refused to be a product. Gentry was one of the first women in Country Rock to produce her own material. She wrote 'Mississippi Delta' in 1967, and it's incredible. It has this amazing arrangement and inventive, playful lyrics. It's so well done and produced. Gentry was one of a kind and broke a lot of barriers in Country Rock. And with that rebellion came a lot of pushback from the record companies. But if you're selling records they're not going to complain all that much. If you're *not* selling records and you're trying to do your own thing, they're gonna have more control over you, because you don't have a leg to stand on... *yet*. But once you do have a leg to stand on, then all of a sudden Ma Rainey's not ugly any more; suddenly she's the Queen of the Blues.

*

Mama Cass – aka Cass Elliot, née Ellen Naomi Cohen – seemed to spend her entire career battling against the perception of an acceptable Pop star image. In the Sixties, women like Twiggy, Nico and Cher were splashed about television and magazines. Cass was the absolute antithesis of what was being sold as sexy. Here was this plus-size woman who had a tendency for excess – in many areas – and she was just awesome. She looked great and she sounded great. As soon as she opened her mouth, she backed it up. She'd always had a pretty stunning voice, but then she got hit on the head by a pipe in a freak accident at a club, and – in that weird way the body has – after the accident her range had increased by three notes.

Mama Cass was the one in The Mamas & the Papas who could really sing; the other guys were all right, but she was the star. She was the one that went on to influence a generation of singers. Anthony Kiedis told *Rolling Stone* in 2002, 'There have been times when I've been very down and out in my life, and the sound of her voice has sort of given me a reason to want to carry on.' Other people who cite her influence include k d lang and Boy George, who proclaimed Cass to be 'the greatest white female singer ever'. She definitely transcended her pain, and you could hear that in her music. In any great singer, you hear that. With Janis you hear that, with Billie Holiday you hear that. Holiday was playing with personal problems from day one and she managed to keep it going as long as she could. Music helped her keep going for a time. And that's why we still talk about people like Mama Cass and Billie Holiday. You put the record on, and it doesn't matter how old it is, it still has a sound and an emotion that touches you.

Everybody knows 'California Dreamin'' (incidentally, Bobby Womack did a version of it that's really amazing and you should check it out if you haven't already): it's one of those songs that takes you there. I mean, even in a frosty and freezing Somerset in England, if I look out the window and play 'California Dreamin'', I get a little warmer. 'California Dreamin'' summons the image we all have of the Golden State: palm trees and sunshine and movie stars and beaches and all that nice stuff. But there's a lot more to Cass Elliot than 'California Dreamin'' and 'Dream a Little Dream of Me'; search out Mama Cass and listen to '(If You're Gonna) Break Another Heart', 'Words of Love', 'That Song' and 'California Earthquake'.

There was a community of musicians that would hang out in Southern California. They did that in New York too, but in Cali they hung out a bit more and played a little bit more music together, and that's how supergroups like Crosby, Stills, Nash & Young came about. That was the first supergroup. Being in Southern California, Mama Cass was surrounded by the top musicians of the day, who would hang out at her house. Joni Mitchell wrote a bunch of songs in her living room and on any given day you might see Eric Clapton playing guitar with David Crosby and Buddy Miles. I imagine people were drawn to Mama Cass because she was incredibly charismatic and larger than life. She lived her life like she was Aretha Franklin. Aretha was her role model in a lot of ways, but also being in the Bay Area at that time, hanging out with the Grateful Dead and doing drugs had a big effect. She would hang out with the Rockers and with the Blues musicians and the Jazz dudes, because all of the cool cats of that time were like, 'That girl can sing. That girl got pipes.'

One of the things that made The Mamas & the Papas great was Mama Cass; this wild woman of Rock 'n' Roll who would party with the Hells Angels and hang out with anybody who would hang out with her. And there were stories going around that people tried to quash: that she was hanging out with black musicians, or perhaps the emphasis was really on black men. Interracial relationships at that point were still very taboo, even though the Bay Area was very liberal.

Mama Cass was into the music, as a way, I think, to mask her physical insecurities. She wasn't necessarily 'beautiful' in the traditional sense that we think of beauty nowadays. But as Tolstoy once wrote, 'It is amazing how complete is the delusion that beauty is goodness.' It's pretty pertinent in that Mama Cass was probably one of the best singers that came out of that generation, and yet she's often completely overlooked. She's known as the big woman who choked to death on a sandwich. You rarely, if ever, see Mama Cass in the 'Best Female Singer' lists – they're usually filled with the likes of Madonna.

Mama Cass was different to so many Pop stars today; her self-image wasn't bound to narcissism. Back then you couldn't go and have your tummy stapled or have plastic surgery and fillers and Botox as you pleased. Back then, it was a case of: 'You are who you are. Make the best of it.' And Mama Cass did, in a lot of ways. As a musician, she was far above and beyond a lot of the popular music that was coming out in that period with female singers. I mean – she had the voice.

Image is all these days, and luckily Mama Cass wasn't subjected to trolls on social media or the 'Best/Worst-Dressed Lists' in magazines. And it's not that Mama Cass didn't look great – she did. She dressed really nicely, in the style of the era, and in that way she became an icon. She'd rock around in her multicoloured kaftans, refusing to conform to Pop star convention of the day. Her hippy style overshadowed that of her more conventionally pretty bandmate Michelle Phillips. Back in 1967, Mama Cass posed naked – except for a few strategically placed daisies – on the cover of a short-lived counterculture magazine called *Cheetah*. I guess in some ways the public decides who is and isn't iconic, but there are people like Mama Cass who become iconic *despite* us and our prescriptive ideas of what's iconic and what's not.

I remember reading a *Time Out* review a few years ago of an album of ours that began 'The increasingly rotund Huey Morgan...' It had nothing whatsoever to do with the album. Back then I was in my early thirties, so I didn't worry about being Mr Gutly Mutly. I was just like, 'Wow. That's a cheap shot that they're taking.' But if you're an 18-year-old with self-esteem issues or worries about your weight, you might not have the emotional capabilities to deal with that. It's a review of the album; it shouldn't be a review of someone's physical appearance. A lot of magazines have a tendency to do that now, because it gets people to read the article and I suppose it in some ways makes us feel better about ourselves. If you say something derogatory about somebody, great, it causes controversy. Nowadays, the artist will get on Twitter and say, 'Fuck you, you misogynist', and the blogger or the magazine can cop themselves a load of free publicity. Before the advent of social networks, it was harder for people to get a rise out of celebrities; it was harder still to be able to directly access them in any meaningful way. Nowadays, an artist can scroll through their timeline and see exactly how many people think they're a fat, lazy, untalented son of a bitch!

When people start saying, 'You're really talented, but you could lose fifty pounds and you'd be really, really, really famous', it's going to take its toll. Mama Cass was a big woman, but so was Aretha Franklin, and plenty of other women who weren't getting the stick that she was. It seems to me that, for the most part, the white half of popular music, as opposed to the black half, was tougher on a woman's looks. Michelle Phillips, Twiggy, Cher... Mama Cass really stood out in a sea of skinny beauties. But that was the dichotomy that made it work – where Michelle could sing wispy harmonies, Mama Cass was the meat of it. It's weird that that kind of stuff was going on even before we could imagine A&R getting involved and fucking things up. It's why I think it's important that – regardless what you think of their music – we do have a handful of female acts like Adele, or Susan Boyle or even crazy Lady Gaga, who challenge the common aesthetic of the accepted Pop star image.

It came to me recently just *how* malignant we are as a society and as consumers. You can be entertained by Tom Waits, who's not conventionally good-looking, but interesting-looking because he's a man. If Tom Waits were a woman, people would be like, 'She's ugly.' It's such a sexist narrative that's been taken with music and these women that were so talented. People who weren't attractive and yet still backed it up are the important part of what I'm getting at here. Because it's one thing to make it if you're hot and talented – it's quite another if you're old or fat or considered unattractive.

Look at Left Eye: she wasn't conventionally pretty – she was cute. She was a wild-ass crazy girl from the South, burning people's houses down and running wild. But TLC broke ground in a lot of ways. You had the huge AIDS epidemic that had started in the Eighties and they came out wearing condoms on their jackets and condoms over their eyes. It was a huge statement. No one did that before and at first they didn't play that stuff in the daytime, because there were kids watching TV and they didn't want people to see condoms. And there was a big thing in America about birth control and people were bombing abortion clinics back then. As any sensible person would tell you, it is a woman's right to choose what she does with her body under those circumstances. You gotta be in that person's shoes. And if you don't have a uterus, shut the fuck up.

Mama Cass almost killed herself by doing those crazy crash diets. She did a string of dates at Caesars Palace in Vegas in 1968 and went on a diet for six months before. She made herself so sick that she was basically unable to perform. She got some pretty crappy reviews. I guess after that, she got to the point of 'Look, I am who I am – I'm just going to do what I'm going to do', and almost did it twice as much. She went back to Vegas in '73 and absolutely slayed that time. When she died in '74, it was during a two-week sold-out residency at the London Palladium.

I think people made Mama Cass feel so bad about her outside that her inside suffered. I think that's why she eventually just didn't give a fuck. Now she's known for the myth of how she died, though she actually died of a heart attack. (In a strange twist of fate, Mama Cass died in the same London flat that Keith Moon would later die in as well. The Mayfair residence, which was near Apple Records, the Playboy Mansion and Tramps, belonged to the singer, Harry Nilsson, who often lent his flat to friends when he was on tour.) But still her Google search is reduced to 'Mama Cass ham sandwich', which woefully negates who she was as a woman, as a singer, as an icon of the Sixties. Mama Cass was chased into her grave, leaving the rest of us to wonder what might have happened if she was still around today. One woman who faced similar unpleasantness about her appearance, and lived to tell the tale – and damn how she told it – was Nina Simone. Every time I hear a particular piano riff, I know I'm going to have a good time for three minutes. Simone (born Eunice Kathleen Waymon in 1933), the High Priestess of Soul truly offered something different.

*

BREAKING THE RULES

Nina Simone's daughter was understandably upset when a comparatively pale-skinned, more narrow-featured actress was cast to depict her mother in a recent biopic, citing two other actresses 'with beautiful, luscious lips and wide noses, and who know their craft' who would have been more appropriate for the role. Another instance, as she and many others saw it, of the imposition of an 'acceptable' form of black beauty. Crazy to think these problems still rage on, and that it can affect as legendary a performer as Nina Simone.

Simone was a natural on the piano and she learnt to play by ear at three years old. She played in church, though she didn't really sing at that point. She got into Bach, Brahms and Beethoven via her music teacher, Muriel Mazzanovich, an Englishwoman who had moved to Simone's hometown of Tryon, North Carolina. Later on, she won a scholarship to Juilliard and then applied to the Curtis Institute of Music in Philadelphia. The Curtis Institute turned down her application – Simone later said she felt it was on grounds of racism, something the Institute denies – and with it dashed her dreams of becoming a prominent African-American classical pianist. She began teaching and, to supplement her income, auditioned to sing and play piano at a bar in Atlantic City. Nina Simone, singer and pianist, was born.

That combination of rigid structure teamed with a sense of adversity made for a powerful combination, because she had the rules down, and the knowledge and desire to smash them. And that's what Nina Simone did. Classical music is very regulated: you can only play at a certain tempo or in a certain key and you can't adjust the key a quarter-tone up. You can play it with feeling though, and Simone was the queen of feel when it came to piano. She took that feeling and used it in a medium where she could really cut loose. Whatever she was singing – whether a song of her own or a standard of the day – you knew immediately it was Nina Simone, for instance, the Gershwin-penned song from 1935, 'I Loves You, Porgy', from *Porgy & Bess*. She created a very singular version. You can list all the people – Billie, Janis, Etta – who sang standards like 'Summertime' or 'My Funny Valentine' or 'Stardust', but you listen to Nina's version of 'Summertime' or 'I Loves You, Porgy' and you understand why she chose it; because she had a new angle on it, she added something to it. If you think of 'My Baby Just Cares For Me', you don't think of Count Basie or Nat King Cole. You think of Nina Simone.

Nina Simone was always 'on the one' – an expression that musicians use to demonstrate that another musician knows what the fuck they're doing. Sure, she might have been drunk sometimes and talked some shit and maybe skipped a note, but everybody's allowed a couple of those days. To have an off day for 0.1 per cent of your life isn't too bad going.

They say Nina used men a lot for sex, like that's such a bad thing, when every other Rock dude in history did the same thing. Some bands would have a system in place. They'd go to the roadie and say, 'Row B12, blonde, red top', and the guy would go and get her. Nina, apparently, would do the same thing; she'd pick up dudes at shows. What a person. If you're that charismatic – and she was – you'd be crazy if you were a red-blooded heterosexual man to not want to spend some time with her. She was magnetic; she had that light. That's why we call them stars.

So multifarious was Simone's output, it became impossible to categorize her. Her sets would include children's songs, original compositions, standards, classical piano. She embodied the spirit of Folk, Jazz, Soul, the Blues. 'It was difficult [for critics] because I was playing popular songs in a classical style with a classical piano technique influenced by cocktail jazz,' she said in *I Put a Spell on You*, her 1992 autobiography. 'On top of that I included spirituals and children's songs [which became] identified with the folk movement. It gave the critics problems...'

Simone wasn't just an exemplary player; she was an orator, a griot, a storyteller and a politician, of sorts. Her take on popular music was to rebel against all the things she had had to learn as a young woman. But perhaps even more key, to rebel against an America that was inherently racist. She revelled in the fact that she was 'allowed' to speak her mind as a black woman at that time. She was beholden to no one, so she could do whatever she wanted and she backed it up on stage. She had a bigger white audience at the time than the Motown guys did, because she came up through the Jazz/Lincoln Center/ liberal white New York audience. She had people that would listen to her because she was good at what she did and she had some big hits. When she played live, she would talk in between songs, almost to the point of excess. You can watch *Live in Montreal* to get an idea of what I'm talking about. She was from the South playing to a mostly white audience and she would ask questions like, 'You guys believe in this black back-of-the-bus stuff?' It would polarize a lot of the crowd but at the same time they all came to see her anyway. This was before the cult of personality, but they loved her music so they would give her five minutes in between songs to tell a story about what the song meant.

Simone is credited with writing the first civil-rights song to be recorded, with 'Mississippi Goddam'. She was a rebel, a restless spirit and an activist who used her innate talent not only to move the masses musically, but also to inspire them.

*

Ruth Brown was to the business of music what Nina was to its spiritual heart. In the Eighties, it was Brown who helped other musicians see just how much they had been ripped off over the years.

As a singer she broke boundaries too. Aretha Franklin was known as the Queen of Soul, and Ruth Brown was the Queen of R&B. Some said R&B stood as much for 'Ruth Brown' as it did for Rhythm & Blues. Little Richard cited her as a key influence on his own vocal style and, when Brown died in Las Vegas at the age of 78, Bonnie Raitt hailed her as one of the original divas. This woman made Atlantic Records so much money that in its early years it was referred to as 'the house that Ruth built'. She's not a name you hear as often as Ella or Aretha or Nina, but Brown was the biggest-selling black female artist of the early Fifties. She dominated the charts with a string of hits, including 'Teardrops From My Eyes', 'So Long', 'I Don't Know', and 'This Little Girl's Gone Rockin''. One of my favourites is 'Too Many Men', which is a brilliantly sharp song about Brown struggling to choose between the various suitors in her life.

Brown pretty much left the business in the Sixties to raise her children, but she popped up here and there, including as an actress in

John Waters's *Hairspray*. Her most significant return, though, was in 1987, when she came back to fight for her rights and for those of other musicians. Her business accountant had made it known to Brown that she hadn't been paid enough dough since she first signed. Brown saw that the labels had been getting an 80:20 split during the cash cow of her early career, and she challenged it. She began to speak out in interviews so passionately and so regularly that eventually Atlantic capitulated; at their 40th birthday at Madison Square Garden, they agreed to pay Brown and 35 other musicians retroactive royalties. Atlantic also contributed around $1.5m to the Rhythm & Blues Foundation, which was set up to help musicians in need.

That was one of the first instances of any musician – male or female – taking the reins of their own career and understanding the business side of it. That was a real crucial break in the business of music. Of course, I'm sure Brown got the usual sexist bullshit because she 'dared' to open her mouth. If a guy is assertive he's a go-getter; if a girl is assertive she's a bitch. But she stood up for her business because she didn't want to get screwed. This was a woman who had grown up in North Carolina in the Thirties picking cotton; she wasn't afraid to get her hands dirty for what she believed in. Because of Brown, not only did her contemporaries benefit, but it also gave other musicians, like me, the opportunity to wise up.

Business acumen aside, Ruth Brown was simply an incredible singer and performer. If you want to check her out, go to YouTube, but make sure you have some really good speakers, because this woman could sing and you need to hear it right.

*

MAKING THE CROSSOVER

Another often-overlooked yet incredibly important figure in music was Celia Cruz, the voice of a Latino generation. We tend to ignore a lot of Salsa and Mambo, especially in Europe. But in Latin America – which is pretty much all those little islands in the Caribbean, and Central America, and even South America – they produce music and musicians that are as good as or better than a lot of the people that we call icons or legends now.

Born to a household of 14 children in a small working-class barrio in Havana, Cuba, in 1925, Celia Cruz came from nothing. I mean, no shoes – nothing. Stupid poor. Her first pair of shoes, in fact, came from a tourist whom she sang for on the streets of Havana. Celia's dad wanted his daughter to seek a steady income as a teacher, but she refused, insisting on becoming a singer after her aunt took her to sing in cabarets all over the city. It all worked out A-OK with Daddy dearest in the end, though, as Cruz would point out in later years: 'I have fulfilled my father's wish to be a teacher as, through my music, I teach generations of people about my culture and the happiness that is found in just living life. As a performer, I want people to feel their hearts sing and their spirits soar.'

Cruz studied at Cuba's Conservatory of Music and took that operatic style and classical learning to the sound of Salsa in the Forties. She was often referred to as the 'Latin Ella Fitzgerald' because of the way she scatted over Salsa. Cruz was also similar to Nina Simone in that she took existing ideas and put her own spin on them. She'd take a standard or a classic and give it the Cruz treatment. In 1950, she was tapped to join a popular Cuban band, La Sonora Matancera, and from there she became a regular figure on the Salsa scene. Celia and her husband left communist Cuba for New York in the Sixties and she would cut a serious shape around Manhattan with her polka-dot dresses, higher-than-high heels and skyscraper wigs. Another woman considered an unconventional beauty, the woman stood out a mile.

Cruz was the only female in the Fania All-Stars, a group of highly skilled Salsa musicians that included Willie Colón, Rubén Blades and Ray Barretto. Being in the All-Stars exposed Cruz to an international audience and she took her music and her positive message to the masses, where she became loved, adored and worshipped by Latin Americans all over the world. You mix that experience of growing up poor in Cuba, the classical training of a music conservatory, and the energy of New York in the Sixties and Seventies, and you're bound to get something pretty damn special. Live, Cruz had an incredible, infectious energy and charisma. Her music transcended language; you could feel her spirit whether or not you could speak Spanish. Check out her version of the classic Cuban Folk song 'Guantanamera' and compare it with others to understand why Cruz is such an important vocalist; her offering is almost operatic. Beautiful stuff.

'La Reina' finally made it big with white audiences after the hit movie *The Mambo Kings*, which she made with Tito Puente and Antonio Banderas. She's not as lauded as some of her female contemporaries – say, Donna Summer – but it's Cruz's image that was spray-painted as a mural on the walls of New York, at Houston and Avenue B, and at 103rd and Lexington. Cruz was no slouch in the awards stakes either. Over her 70-plus-album career – during which she only sang in Spanish – she worked with David Byrne and Dionne Warwick, clocked up 23 Gold albums, amassed three Grammys and four Latin Grammys, was awarded a National Medal of Arts by Bill Clinton and received doctorates from Yale and the University of Miami. When she died of brain cancer in 2003 at the age of 77, over 200,000 people went to pay their respects as her body lay in state.

I have a great record of hers that someone put me on to. It's a concert that she did in Cuba in 1953, and it was recorded off the radio. It's just Cruz singing live, and she's amazing. You can hear the static and it fades out and then fades back in, because they're trying to jiggle the wire to get the signal.

Like Mama Cass, Celia Cruz wasn't considered pretty but her voice was undeniably beautiful. And she sang it like it was the Blues before her and Hip-Hop after; she sang about everyday things that people go through: My husband stayed out late and I think he was with another woman. Am I not enough for him?

Celia helped transport Salsa and Latin-American culture into the mainstream at a time when it was totally dominated by men like Tito Puente. She was a lone voice in a field of testosterone, but it was her easy charm and infectious talent that took Cuban music to a global audience.

*

Dusty Springfield, born Mary Isobel Catherine Bernadette O'Brien, is another woman who helped spread a sound; it's incredible to consider that a young white girl from West Hampstead took Soul around the globe.

When she was 11 years old, O'Brien's convent school teacher asked her what she wanted to be when she grew up. 'A Blues singer,' came the precocious reply. Around the same time, O'Brien and two of her school buddies performed a song at the school talent show: Bessie Smith's 'St Louis Blues'. The nuns walked out in horror!

Dusty Springfield carried the Blues in her heart from the start.

To me, Dusty is a true renegade and a rebel heart through and through. When you consider her contemporaries were Cilla Black and Sandie Shaw, Dusty could have easily sold her soul to the Pop charts. White girls making black music was completely unheard of at the time, but she stuck to her guns and made the music that she loved the most.

Springfield was born into a religious family; her tax accountant father had been brought up in India, while her mom hailed from County Kerry, Ireland. The household was fraught with tension between Dusty's pedantic father and slightly more tempestuous mother; there were arguments and lots of plates were thrown at mealtimes – a habit that Dusty and her siblings would apparently continue into their adult lives. Her childhood, she would say in later years, wasn't the happiest.

Despite their eccentricities, Dusty's parents had pretty awesome taste in music. Her dad was a Jazz and Blues fanatic and Dusty was raised on the music of Ella Fitzgerald, Jelly Roll Morton and Peggy Lee. At 12, Dusty wandered into a record store and recorded her first song – a cover of Irving Berlin's 1912 track, 'When the Midnight Choo Choo Leaves for Alabam".

In her late teens, she joined the Lana Sisters, who were pretty edgy for a girl group of that time. They toured with Nat King Cole and had a hit with 'Seven Little Girls Sittin' In The Backseat (Kissin' and Huggin' with Fred)' but Dusty needed more. She needed R&B. She needed Soul. She needed to sing the Blues.

She teamed up with her brother and his friend for a brief spell in a Folk-Soul band called The Springfields. The trio cut a record in Nashville, which had some success, but Dusty finally struck gold when she went solo in 1963. Releasing 'I Only Want To Be With You' later that year, Dusty finally had people's attention; she was ready to show the world her sweet Soul music.

In 1964, Dusty was in Cape Town, South Africa, where she was asked to perform to a segregated audience. Springfield refused. Instead, she performed to an integrated audience, although her tour was cut short and she was all but run out of town. The police escorted Dusty and her band to the airport, as a line of black airport staff formed a guard of honour. Dusty had a real love and understanding of black music. She was the woman to introduce Motown to a wider UK audience in 1965 by hosting a special of the Detroit label on *Ready, Steady, Go!* This would be the first time British audiences got to see The Supremes, The Temptations, Stevie Wonder and Smokey Robinson. It's hard to believe now, but until that broadcast radio wouldn't play those guys and a proposed tour had struggled to sell. After *Ready, Steady, Go!* we saw the Motown revolution. Music, as we knew it, would never be the same.

Dusty was in love with the sound emerging from America and when Atlantic Records – home to Aretha Franklin and Otis Redding – offered her the opportunity to make a record, she was thrilled. Recorded with Jerry Wexler, *Dusty in Memphis* is a seminal record from that era. 'Son of a Preacher Man' came from those sessions, as well as 'Just A Little Lovin'. She had the voice, and the opportunity. Opportunity is a great thing, because you can have it and decide not to take it, for fear of not being able to measure up to the expectations. But Dusty went for hers all the time. If you listen to *Dusty in Memphis* you realize just how hard she went for it. She laid her stall out with that record. Although that record didn't sell – in fact it put her career into a slump for a few years – it's now recognized as being one of the era's true greats.

Dusty Springfield was the true definition of crossover. She sang songs that really connected with people and, if she didn't write the song, she made it her own. Everybody is familiar with *Pulp Fiction* and 'Son of a Preacher Man' but there are some songs on *Dusty in Memphis* that are so deep. You can almost imagine her in the studio, the engineers looking at each other like 'Damn, this girl is good'. She belonged behind the mic. And that's the thing that ties this book together: these are all people who were going for something that was a little bit extra. It wasn't required of them to be popular or successful, they just wanted to make the best music possible in their own unique way. There was a drive to express themselves that I think has been culled over the last decade or two.

In many ways, Dusty contributed to the Northern Soul scene, bringing music back to the UK that she was hearing in Northern

America. People started listening back to Motown records, and that turned into people discovering music on other labels, that real R&B music, which became Northern Soul. If you listen to a lot of Northern Soul, it was records by people that you knew – like the Temptations or the Isley Brothers – but that hadn't had a major release, or wasn't found on a Motown *Greatest Hits*. Though rarely credited, Dusty was responsible for the resurgence in that genre of music. It was a big influence on her growing up and that's why she went out of her way to go to places like Memphis to record. I think that's a cool thing for someone to do. It was the same thing with The Clash: what they loved they immersed themselves in. Nothing else mattered but the music. When it comes to music now, money changes everything. Musicians aspire to being a brand now. Why do you want to be a commercial endeavour when you can be a creative entity? You can't do both at the same time. It's become cool to aspire to being wealthy now, rather than brilliant.

I digress. Dusty is important because she took Soul music to the masses. If you want to hear Dusty at her finest, then you need to listen to the *Memphis* album. That was the highlight of her career. It was revolutionary for the time that a white artist could go to the South and create what Dusty created and be totally accepted by the black audience. She was in the R&B charts at that time; there were no videos so they didn't know if she was black or white; she just sang good. And then when they found out it's like 'Oh, ok. Well, she's awesome, we like her'.

I hope Dusty knew how much she was appreciated. The Pet Shop Boys reminded us how important she was in the late Eighties when they recorded 'What Have I Done To Deserve This' with her, but I wonder if she knew the legacy that she would leave behind. Alongside Nina Simone, Springfield offered a true alternative to the more saccharine sounds of the time. She put her heart and soul, not pounds and pence, into music.

Dusty died, aged 59, on the day she was due to receive her OBE from Buckingham Palace. There seems to be some twisted fate in that; Dusty eventually received her dues, but somehow it was a just a little too late.

✱

In 1970, Janis Joplin, who was a huge fan of Bessie Smith, tracked down the unmarked grave that Smith had been buried in. (Bessie Smith may have been wealthy when she died in 1937, but somehow she ended up in an unmarked grave thanks to her feckless and, by all accounts, greedy ex-husband.) Years later, along with Juanita Green, who had been Smith's housekeeper as a child, Janis paid to have a proper tombstone erected. It's inscribed with the words 'The greatest Blues singer in the world will never stop singing'.

In a way, that unmarked grave symbolizes the unacknowledged women of the Blues. If you look at what Bessie Smith, Ma Rainey and all these incredible Blues women gave us, we should all be paying our dues: they are where it all started; they sowed the seeds for everything that was to come.

ROCKIN'
'N'
ROLLIN'

Ironically, the people we call our icons of Rock – Jimi Hendrix, Janis Joplin, Jim Morrison, James Brown, Joe Strummer and more – were iconoclasts during their lifetimes. They raged against the establishment; they risked their lives for their music. Frank Sinatra was the original Rock star, James Brown brought the Funk and Hendrix made the guitar sing.

You don't aspire to be an icon if you're a musician. It's a crown you try to dodge, especially nowadays, because the spotlight burns your soul while the paps are outside your house or chasing you down on motorbikes.

For me, the real icons are those people who upended the status quo, people who rocked our world so hard it shattered. Like Bo Diddley. He did a lot of rule-breaking and not enough people give him credit for it. He created an entire rhythm that people use today. My band used it on our track, 'Korean Bodega'; a lot of people use the Bo Diddley beat. That was his signature. Bo Diddley took the Blues and turned it into Rock 'n' Roll. Because of Diddley, we have The Who and The Stones, Hendrix and Pink Floyd.

B B King's another one: he started out as a radio DJ before creating a whole new way of playing the guitar. He was inspired by Blind Lemon Jefferson and T-Bone Walker, popularizing what would be his signature left-hand vibrato and vocal-like string bends. King's style of playing became part of the Rock guitar player's lexicon, including the likes of Jeff Beck and George Harrison. He would do these huge extended solos that we would see musicians replicating for years to come. This guy loved – I should say loves, he's still alive and kickin', playing hundreds of shows a year – the guitar so much that he once ran back into a burning dance hall to save his $30 Gibson guitar, which he later named Lucille.

Guys like these are rightful icons because they suffused our culture with something other than music: it was an ideology, a movement, a way of life.

*

A NEW RELIGION

It's perhaps no coincidence that we use the word icon, with its religious connotations, to describe the greats of popular culture. The way I see it, music is the religion of this millennium. When Lennon told the *London Evening Standard,* 'The Beatles are more popular than Jesus', he was dead right. Back when he said that, in the Sixties, Christianity was in decline, with kids worshipping The Beatles far more than they did Jesus. This was the Baby Boom generation; they didn't want to sit in church all Sunday. They wanted to listen to Rock 'n' Roll and dance and make out with each other.

When Christianity started to decline in the UK, you had these four guys waiting in the wings to take the place of God. When John, Paul, Ringo and George came on stage to speak to the people, the people would lose their minds – just like they had for Elvis in the States. Music was something we were willing to live and die for. As Lennon prudently pointed out, musicians became our gods, our deities, our idols. We put artists on pedestals and their music replaced the Holy Ghost with a different sense of spirituality. Buying an album and bringing it into your home was almost like bringing home a religious artifact or relic. Kids would pore over the liner notes like they were trying to learn the Bible ahead of Sunday school. Whether it's in a stadium, an arena or a dingy room in the back of a pub, we, the congregation, fervently worship at the altar of Rock 'n' Roll. Of Pop. Of Hip-Hop. Of Folk. Of House. Kids no longer drink the wine and take the body of Christ; they're ingesting horse tranquillizer and Jägerbombs in order to reach a higher plane.

As Christianity went into decline, people looked elsewhere for the gospel and for their gods. Jimi Hendrix, James Brown and Mick Jagger took us to spiritual heaven. Experiencing music became as close to a religious epiphany as you could get outside a place of worship.

When I saw Jeff Buckley live at Sin-é coffeehouse in New York City in 1993, it was a quasi-religious experience. I was blown away. The lights go off and the spotlight comes up on this guy, hunched in the corner with a Strat, and he just starts singing like God. Seeing him live will be something I'll probably remember when my life flashes before my eyes. It'll be my family, and Buckley playing 'Hallelujah'. I remember seeing him live like it was yesterday because it was such an emotional moment, seeing this guy completely expose himself. It was at a nightclub yet people were silent. You could have heard the proverbial pin drop. You got the sense that the audience felt ashamed that they couldn't be as honest with themselves as he was being with us. He created music that even other artists revere and revel in, and to this day go back and listen to. Buckley was so in tune with his emotions that he could write and perform music that was elegiac, transcendent. You know that if he'd been allowed to continue to live, if the universe hadn't taken him away, we would have heard a lot more beautiful music from him.

But maybe it was meant to be. Maybe Buckley was meant to be here for a little while to remind us to be open and honest and to live from the heart. Listening to Jeff Buckley's music can help a person emotionally; it's uplifting in the same way as Martin Luther King Jr, Sly and the Family Stone and Led Zeppelin are. He showed me his entire heart that night, knowing that I could rip it out. But he knew that's what he had to do to get his point across. As a musician, you have to put yourself on the line, bare it all, take a leap – otherwise what's the point? In this sense, music, like religion, makes us feel un-alone, part of a tribe, a band of followers united in our love for an artist or a genre. Certain songs and sounds within songs resonate with us on a deeply spiritual level. We idolize these people for what they do with instruments and words and their voices.

That's why I love music – because it saved my soul.

Music is one of the few things that can transcend nationality, class and colour – aside from religion. Religion was, and is, about getting to the existential essence of who we are as human beings: who we are and why we're here. The God figure – regardless of religion – was historically the creator. 'Let us make man in Our image according to Our likeness.' But now, we are our own creators. We create our own selves by what we wear, what we listen to, by how we talk, how we speak on social issues, how we speak on injustices.

That's why we choose music as our religion – because of our idea that we are the centre of our universe. The Internet's been a positive force in many ways: we can make new discoveries and explore, and spend a lifetime getting into the beautiful things that make us feel special. That's pretty much where we are now as music listeners; we're explorers of ourselves because we are our own universe. I guess time will tell if that's a good thing in the long run or not. It's getting to the point where, whatever we enjoy, there's something holy about it. And that's using an old word to describe a new feeling. But now people often use the expression 'a religious experience', be it sexual, or near-death, or seeing Led Zeppelin live at Madison Square Garden. People freak at music, jumping up and down and acting like crazy people – catching the Holy Ghost, the Holy Spirit. Why do women act fuckin' nuts at a One Direction concert? Same reason they acted nuts back in the Forties, when Frank Sinatra was coming up. Hormones. 'Oh my gosh. His lips, his eyes, his hips...'

*

THE BLUEPRINT

The first icon of popular music – our inaugural Rock god – was Frank Sinatra. He became the model upon which we would base all future

Rock stars – he was the first teen idol. Born on 12 December 1915, Frank almost died at birth. The 13½-pound new arrival wasn't breathing – until his auntie grabbed him from the doctor and chucked him under a cold tap. I guess you could say that, from that day forth, Frank Sinatra had that fighting spirit.

Before Frank hit the stage in the late Thirties and early Forties, music was the preserve of parents, and kids had no real interest in it. It wasn't for young people. But with Frank, all of a sudden you had a young guy who related directly to kids – to young girls in particular. They had just gotten through Prohibition when World War II came and all the men went off to Europe. If you were at home, you had the Andrews Sisters and Frank Sinatra. Here was this 24-year-old handsome, cool motherfucker singing to all those kids without daddies. Timing, talent and a sense of style – but more than that, Frank created a market that had yet to exist before his arrival.

When Frank hit the stage, you had all the girls screaming like they would do a decade or two later for The Beatles. Sinatra brought an influx of young people to music. Suddenly these white kids wanted to swing and dance. And thanks to the advent of post-war 'allowances' for kids, they had the money to buy the music they wanted to listen to. That's where the economy came into Rock 'n' Roll, I think. Sinatra got so big in the Fifties that in 1960 he was able to start his own label, Reprise Records. Through Reprise, he put out Sammy Davis Jr, Dean Martin, Bing Crosby, Rosemary Clooney (guess she taught her nephew that slick Rat Pack look)… a whole heap of stars. Frank knew the business and the men with the money – and muscle – to make it work. Sinatra could see label owners were making good money, but he saw the bigger picture. He was smart. Plus he knew the Mob and he knew the accountants of the Mob. He saw what was happening in music and took advice, and, with a little gentle nudging, Frank got his label. The Mob saw they could make a few connections – they were opportunists – they saw a new economy emerging that was legit and they saw a way to launder their money and make a profit. When the Mafia got involved, that's when we saw the advent of 'pay for play': the Mob used their influence to have certain records played on the radio. That's how radio pluggers came about – lots of people were very much in bed with each other. 'Fancy a week in Miami, first class, five-star? Play this for me, wouldja, kid?'

Vice was always entwined with music. The Mob controlled the liquor in America during the time of the Blues. *Boardwalk Empire* is a great depiction of those days. From the beginning, the Mafia and music walked hand in hand. Whenever reality started getting too close to musicians and got in the way of them being Rock 'n' Roll, the Mob would push reality away – forcefully. And with money. That's what talked. When they realized money could be made, that's when they became intertwined. And they still are, to an extent. A lot of guys still know a lot of guys…! Popular music is still super-corrupt, of course – it's just found other ways to do it.

Frank not only enraptured the kids, he was the first one to really understand that he could do what the fuck he wanted. 'I can be friends with the Mob and no one cares? OK, great!' He birthed that full-package Rock 'n' Roll mentality. He may have married his childhood sweetheart, Nancy, but Sinatra went out with every girl that looked at him twice and drank as much liquor as he wanted. The Ten Commandments of being a Rock 'n' Roll star were written around Sinatra: sex, drugs, girls, champagne, parties, a little politics. Sinatra was even arrested for his Rock-star ways. In 1938, at the age of 23, he was charged with adultery and seduction for having sex with a single woman 'of good repute'. The charges were dropped when the woman turned out to be married, but his mugshot remains an iconic image and a waypoint that popular music had a new star – and this boy was bad.

Here was the blueprint for the Rock 'n' Roll star, and he got everything effortlessly right. The suit: 'For me, the tuxedo was a way of life,' Frank was known to say. The hair, with or without the toupée, was always super-slick. The cigarette, dangling just so from the lips. The hat, tilted to just the right angle: 'Cock your hat – angles are attitudes.' And people lapped it up. There was Dean Martin and Tony Bennett, but Frank was the first one who got the idea of being a star on that level.

Frank was just that little bit different. He had a certain swagger and was working with a lot of black musicians who brought a little Soul to his swing. He was also unafraid to be an advocate of civil rights. He grew up in Hoboken, right across the water from Manhattan. Hoboken was integrated and so Frank grew up around Jazz musicians, smoking jazz cigarettes – he knew what was going on. He was savvy to it. He grew up round those cats, playing with them, singing in bands with them. Most of the guys in his bands were black. He took Sammy Davis Jr under his wing and said, 'This guy is a fuckin' genius. Because he's black, you're not going to give him any play? That's bullshit.' Here was an Italian guy connected to the Mob who was also connected to the

Civil Rights Movement. That was a pretty out-there thing to do back in the Forties and Fifties. But Frank was the son of immigrants; he came from somewhere else too.

Frank was the original entrepreneur; this guy sang, he danced, he made movies, he owned a record label. Jay Z likes to brag that he created the blueprint. No way. Frank Sinatra is the one, the only, the original full-package Rock 'n' Roller, and it was he who set the path for the Rock 'n' Roll greats to come.

*

THE FUTURE-SEEKER

Doing what the fuck he wanted was something Sinatra had in common with a certain Miles Dewey Davis III. Uncompromising. Exasperating. Stubborn. A mean-spirited son of a bitch. That's what everybody said about Davis but he was a talented bastard and there were no shortage of musicians willing to drop everything to play with him – so he must have been doing something right.

You might be surprised to find a Jazz musician in a chapter about Rock 'n' Roll, but Rock 'n' Roll is about spirit, and it's the only way to define what Miles Davis brought to Jazz music. Miles gets a bad rap for being an obtuse, difficult dude, but he invented a whole new style of Jazz, several times over. He was at the forefront of so many variations: Hard Bop, Bebop, Jazz Fusion. Like Nina Simone, Davis was classically trained and also a hard-headed dude – meaning he too took great intellectual joy in disrupting the rigid ideologies of what he'd been taught as a child prodigy – in his case in Illinois and later as student at New York's Juilliard. Miles tore up the rulebook, and with such style.

He only took a place at Juilliard to be in the same city as his hero, Charlie Parker, whom he eventually met. Through Parker, Miles got a lesson in life: they roomed together, took drugs together and played together. Ultimately, Miles would replace Dizzy Gillespie in Parker's quintet. Not a bad schooling, right? Consider the musicians Davis played with over the years: Parker, Dizzy Gillespie, Thelonious Monk, Sonny Rollins, Billy Eckstine, J J Johnson... I guess it's little surprise that Miles would be as revolutionary, rebellious and Rock 'n' Roll as he was.

Miles released 48 studio albums, 36 live albums and countless box sets, bootlegs and compilations. He was always in the studio, rehearsing or playing live. He was a perfectionist – seemingly to the point of OCD – in every area of life. He was always meticulous about how he dressed, keeping himself immaculate at all times.

I mean, this is a guy who quit Juilliard because he thought they were backwards, that they couldn't teach him anything. That was what was cool about him – that's a rebellious thing for a young, middle-class man to do, and to know that he had that in him to do it. Just as he became known as the Father of Modern Jazz, he shrugged that off and created Fusion Jazz, then shrugged that off and started putting electric guitars and other electric instruments into his music. He kept reinventing himself. People say Madonna reinvents herself – she doesn't, she rebrands herself. Miles actually altered the course of music – multiple times. He could play whatever was in his head, and that's very rare.

And I don't think it was drugs, either, that made him go to those places. Miles was one of those innately talented people who just have it. I'm sure he got high, but not to the extent of addiction like Charlie Parker, Thelonious Monk or even Wes Montgomery, a great guitarist notorious for taking heroin. Miles had a brief heroin period but he moved on from it. He walked the line and decided ultimately that drugs were holding him back, not lifting him up. He could see people around him dying and he was smart – no one could ever accuse Miles Davis of being stupid.

Miles really came into the mainstream consciousness with *Birth of the Cool,* his album showcasing this new style of Jazz, with Coltrane and Monk beside him – he had everybody following in his footsteps. Even laymen who aren't Jazz heads can listen to *Birth of the Cool* and recognize it as Jazz as we now know it. Up to then, Count Basie and Duke Ellington were doing traditional kinds of Jazz. Miles introduced all of this weird atonal stuff, mixing with musicians like Monk – who was definitely a freak of nature and a brilliant, brilliant musician. I have all these recordings of Monk just playing piano by himself – the most beautiful stuff, but I have no idea where the brother is coming from. I just can't place it. It's everything at once. It's like the space–time continuum theory. It's like everything exists at once; it's a world wrapped up in this coil. And he played with Miles – he wanted to play with him – so together they created these ephemeral masterpieces.

To say 'This is the birth of cool', that's a bold statement. Miles talked all this shit but he backed it up; he was on the one. Then came *Bitches Brew*; 'Pharaoh's Dance' is a fucking masterpiece. All the hottest dudes were lining up to play with Miles then. He was kind of an oracle. You can talk to a lot of people about him, and I have – especially Jazz heads in New York – and they will all tell you he was a jerk. He didn't like people coming up and talking to him when he was out. He was a mean drunk. But he stayed around for so long and never let up on trying to push the boundaries.

Davis broke the traditions of Jazz. He took the crystal ball that people were looking into for 40 years or so and just smashed it. He didn't even look back; he just threw it over his shoulder, took his trumpet with him and played whatever he wanted to. That included a lot of stuff that was dismissed by the Jazz traditionalists as atonal (i.e. with no melody), but there was a lot of melody and there was Blues, there was improvisation... There was a lack of improvisation before Miles. Before him, you could play 64-bar solos, people were singing over songs or playing stuff people could dance to, but this guy was throwing that out. He really did shift everyone's idea of what Jazz was and what Jazz could be.

That was revolutionary at the time – it was the new classical music at that time in America. Jazz came from the Blues, and at first people tended to play stuff from the Benny Goodman school of Swing, with Duke Ellington and Louis Armstrong. Then Miles Davis came in, in the same way that Punk Rock did later – and the way he did it was so influential. Those recordings are mostly one-takes. He didn't multi-track stuff. Back in the Fifties he couldn't. It was just Miles in a studio with his trumpet and his brain. That's what Miles Davis was. He was a big brain. He put all these guys to shame and changed things up in a lasting way.

Blues artists could see how Miles Davis was influenced by them, and in turn it influenced how Blues guitar players played – a lot of Blues guitar players started doing Jazz Fusion post-Miles. He'd created this idea of Jazz Fusion. Davis kept putting these benchmarks down. Look at Q-Tip and Ali from A Tribe Called Quest; decades after Davis they were sampling all of their grandpas' or their uncles' Jazz records and it gave them so many ideas.

Davis influenced a lot more people than he's given credit for. Lonnie Liston Smith had the idea for 'Expansions', one of the best dance records ever made. Whatever kind of dance music you like, you have to know Lonnie Smith and you have to know 'Expansions'. It features all Jazz musicians playing – there's no electric musicians; it's all Smith's Jazz buddies from Miles's band. And it's sampled the hell out of by rappers, from elders like Jay Z to newbies like Chance the Rapper and Joey Bada$$. Popular music started to have overt Jazz influence, and overt Hip-Hop influences, from the Eighties onwards. You can hear it in Dave Grohl's drumming, for instance. He grew up in DC listening to Hip-Hop and he brought it to Nirvana.

People don't really listen to Jazz nowadays, which is sad. But listen to someone like Christian Scott – he's incredible. He has a record called *Christian aTunde Adjuah*, which is this really great, socially conscious album. You can tell he's very influenced by Miles. When people say Wynton Marsalis took the flame from Miles Davis, he didn't – he wears smart suits and plays Carnegie Hall! That's not Miles Davis. There's cool and then there's fakin' the funk – guys like Kenny G. They're fucking it up for people who liked saxophone!

That's one of the things you don't hear about Miles. He took guys like Lonnie in, gave them street cred, then let them go off and do their thing – and he went on to the next thing. One thing Miles hated was going back to his old music; once he'd put the record out he didn't want to play it. That's why he had the reputation for being an asshole, because he was playing stuff he didn't want to play any more. Whenever you see him playing live in the Sixties, he looks pissed off. Because he was playing stuff that he shouldn't – to his mind – have been playing.

Look at the number of records Davis had in the Jazz charts; he sold a lot of records to a lot of folks. *Kind of Blue* did over four million copies in the US alone; so influential that it was made a national treasure by the US House of Representative on its 50th anniversary in 2009. I bought *Birth of the Cool* when I was trying to re-educate myself. I found the Blues in it because he was doing a freeform type of expression. Miles and the musicians that played on *Birth of the Cool* like J J Johnson and Al Haig were tight but able to play loose at the same time. They were willing to put one foot in outer space, pretty much. It's like hearing *Planet Rock* for the first time as a Hip-Hop head – it was the same thing. Once you hear it, you know that, wow, this is something completely amazing that I've never heard before. And will never hear quite the same again.

✱

THE SHOWMEN

Someone else you might not strictly think of as Rock 'n' Roll in terms of his music, but who helped shape our notions of Rock 'n' Roll behaviour and attitude, is the late, great James Brown. He was pretty wild: car chases, drugs, messing with women – but people still loved him; he still got to play at the White House. Now *that* is Rock 'n' Roll.

I talked to one of Hip-Hop's true greats recently, Afrika Bambaataa, and he told me about working with the King of Soul, James Brown. 'It was powerful doing this record with JB called "Unity",' the Zulu Nation leader and breakbeat DJ originator said. 'The idea of the record was to tell people that you must have unity with yourself in order to have unity with each other on this great planet. And working with James was powerful in learning how to write lyrics; seeing the respect and getting an understanding of life itself. James had an understanding of what he needed to go through and struggled to be the hardest-working man in show business. He knew every note of every song. James Brown was *on the* one. That's what he gave us. When he said 'downbeat' you brought it down; when he said 'upbeat' you knew to bring it up. He was a very powerful musician and understood the groove. Truthfully, the whole music industry would stink if it wasn't for James Brown.'

Bam is right. James had this thing about him. I've played with Pee-Wee Ellis, who was in the James Brown Revue, a couple of times and he and his band are always completely on the one. They knew exactly where they were at every moment, at any given time in the song, whether performing or recording. And James Brown was on the one. That's what made him so special; everything he did was 'James Brown'. You could tell immediately when you heard a James Brown record that it was a James Brown record.

There wouldn't be Funk without James Brown. To me, he's the King of Soul, not the Godfather – I get *The Godfather* reference, but he wasn't a godfather looking after people's kids when they died. James was the King of Soul, Aretha was the Queen of Soul.

I spend a lot of time on YouTube watching James Brown performances. There are so many great ones: Paris in 1967, where he does a nine-minute version of 'It's a Man's Man's Man's World'. Even by James Brown standards, it was such an epic performance. He had his whole band there, he was in his element and his band were so tight. He was sweating, sweating, sweating. He came with it. You knew he was probably fucked up on PCP or whatever else, but he came with it. Not only musically, but his performances were also ridiculously iconic. He'd hit the stage with his hair in rollers and a lime-green jumpsuit and you'd know James Brown was in town. The whole schtick with the cape and the back-and-forth with his musical director – 'I can't take no more.' 'James, come off stage, you gonna die, you given 'em too much.' The crowd loved it. Show business was also about entertainment and it still is. But now it's show *business* and it's not Rock 'n' Roll. It started off as show business when Frank Sinatra broke the mould and made it the music business; because it was still about the music at that point.

We wouldn't have the inclination to be funky without James. The stuff he did with his band, the Famous Flames; you could hear something really different was happening to music. No other band was really making it so damn funky. Allen Toussaint was doing his thing down in New Orleans, but it was James who really 'took it to the bridge'. When JB hit it, he hit it big. He created the idea of Soul music and Soul power, and changed the entire course of music; the 'Funky Drummer' beat is still heard in almost every Hip-Hop song. Every bullshit David Guetta house remix, you hear a James Brown sample in there somewhere.

James came from a church background. The gospel beat of music being played in a lot of these churches in the South crept into his songs. He was one of the first people to take that beat and slow it down. That's where the Funk was; the Funk is God. He not only created a new genre of music but was also fully in control of it. It wasn't a producer-based set-up where he was being directed and told what to do. People got behind James Brown for lots of reasons – because of the songs he wrote, and sang, and played, and produced. He was the guy producing, arranging, writing and getting someone from the horn section to do stabs. He didn't formally write music, he did it innately. When Bam said 'Music wouldn't have been fun without James Brown', he's right, it wouldn't have been. It wouldn't have been funky either.

Being on the one, Brown always knew exactly what bar he was in; he would even fine his band if they made mistakes on stage. Bernard Purdie, who played drums for The 3B's and played several sessions with James Brown, told me a great story about how he got fined for once hitting the beat wrong. Or so James thought, but it was actually the percussionist who had made the mistake. Brown insisted Purdie pay the fine of $25 or whatever it was, but Purdie refused, pointing out that he hadn't made the mistake. Once Brown realized, he came to Purdie: 'Stay, I'll tell 'em you paid me.' Purdie said, 'No, don't tell 'em I paid you because it wasn't my mistake, it was the percussion player and I'm not paying you. You're not getting your $25. I'm going to play with Aretha.' So he was Aretha's drummer for a while until James came back and had to say sorry, which was unheard of. James Brown never had to apologize for shit. His rules were that he never said sorry.

James was not only one of the greatest entertainers of our time, but also one of music's foremost activists. Although he was reluctant to overtly reference race in his music, he performed at numerous civil rights benefits during the Sixties. He had the consciousness of Black America in his mind in every song that he wrote from the mid-Sixties through the Seventies. Throughout the Civil Rights Movement, James was heavily into Black Power and all about people getting down with the programme – as they should. He was such an icon, not only to black folks but to white folks too when he started to cross over. He later called his song 'Say It Loud – I'm Black and I'm Proud' obsolete, insisting that people shouldn't be defined by race. But back then, black people were still referred to as 'coloured' or 'Negroes'. Here was a song that asserted black pride ferociously, and both the song and Brown remain enduring symbols of black pride.

James was a pretty righteous guy. 'Down and Out in New York City' tells the story of a guy trying to survive in New York City during the winter. People don't know that song off the cuff, perhaps, but it's from the soundtrack to the movie *Black Caesar*. It's a great song and it shows James being empathetic and also telling a story that people can relate to. Another great track is 'Take Some, Leave Some', the third song from '73's *Payback* album, which is about the drugs on the tour bus. It's seven-and-a-half minutes long. 'Take some, but leave some for me… The pantry is full and it has enough for all of us but don't wipe me out.' 'I Don't Want Nobody to Give Me Nothing' was about relying on yourself and creating your own opportunities in life. Brown wrote a song in the Sixties called 'Don't Be a Drop-Out', in an attempt to inspire young people to continue in education. Education was a big concern for Brown, who had to drop out of school at 12 for 'insufficient clothing'. He was simply too poor to afford appropriate clothing for school.

As a songwriter, he mentioned his background and his life so much in his music that you could instantly relate to him if you were from a desperate background. That's what made the music so interesting. That's why you would buy his records – not only because you liked it, but because you identified with it. James Brown and his music spoke right to you.

Brown grew up during the Great Depression in extreme poverty in South Carolina. After the divorce of his parents, he went to live with his aunt, who ran a brothel. It's safe to say he probably saw a few things. As a kid, he did what he had to do to make a nickel. He would pick cotton, he would shine shoes for sailors, he would dance for them. He used to tell the story of how he didn't have underwear from a store until he was nine years old; before then he made do with underpants fashioned out of sacks. After being kicked out of school aged 12, he lived a certain duality. He sang in church but inevitably, perhaps, due to his abject circumstances, he turned to crime. He did three years in prison from the age of 16 for stealing a car. But it was in the slammer that he met the late, great Bobby Byrd; and his life as a musician really began.

If it weren't for James Brown, music would be very different. When you look at Brown, you see a guy who had a lot of covering up to do. You could see that there was a lot he was hiding. A deep insecurity is evident in many of the greats: Brown, Joplin, Mama Cass… Everyone had their hole to fill, for whatever reason, and some used drugs to fill it.

Deep down – and this happens with a lot of the musicians that we're talking about who were raised in the church – there's an inherent guilt complex at play. They know they're doing wrong and they still do it anyway, because that's how they got to be James Brown in the first place. That's how he came to be on the one. It didn't matter necessarily if you were a believer or not, because it was instilled in you at a young age and was therefore in your conscience – and that's going to manifest itself. At the time James was growing up, people were more religious in general. It was an accepted part of everyday life: church on a Sunday, Sunday school, religious iconography all over homes. In the UK today, plenty of people identify as Jewish or Muslim or Roman Catholic, but people don't go to church like they did. At that point in time, spirituality in communities and therefore in music was ingrained. James Brown had his battles in life – some of them very publicly – but he still brought us Funk and Soul. And he always brought it on the one.

He may have passed on, but it is true to say that the King of Soul, the icon of Funk, still lives on.

*

PLAYING TO A DIFFERENT BEAT

It was during the Sixties and Seventies that musicians started to get more props. A lot of that came from James Brown and the Funky Drummer: 'Let the drummer get some – turn it loose!', he'd shout. And of course that song itself, with drums by Clyde Stubblefield, is one of the most sampled in Hip-Hop and popular music history. Before then, no one ever called out the drummer. James would scream Fred Wesley's name in songs, or 'Yo, Maceo', but no one before then really shouted musicians out. But once people started seeing how hard that shit was, finally musicians started to get their dues.

The Who were a three-piece with a singer; these guys knew what the fuck they were doing. Zak Starkey, who has played with The Who since the Nineties, told me it was really tough playing with them because they were always on the one, always on top of their shit.

In a lot of ways, Keith Moon was to drums what Hendrix was to the guitar. People forget just how great a drummer Keith was because they focus on the crazy stories around him: trashing hotel rooms, blowing up toilets with dynamite, letting his Rolls-Royce coast into a swimming pool (an accident, admittedly). But The Who were a seminal band and Keith was one of the best drummers we've seen. *Rolling Stone* named him the world's second-best drummer of all time, after John Bonham.

You can't just start playing with The Who if you're a day-one drummer or a day-one guitar player. There are so many complicated nuances to the playing of that music that non-musicians don't understand. Some of it is incredibly difficult to play. For instance, Keith Moon didn't play with a high-hat; he just had cymbals all over the place. He was a very busy drummer and he was a drummer's drummer. Danny Goffey from Supergrass reminds me of Moon because he's such an animated drummer. He's really underrated, too.

I didn't really appreciate how great a drummer Keith Moon was until I watched a live The Who concert in my teens. They had shows on American TV like *The Midnight Special* and *Don Kirshner's Rock Concert* that aired after *Saturday Night Live* at 1am. So if you were allowed to stay up, or your mother had gone to bed, you could watch these live shows and discover some incredible musicians. I saw Steve Miller play for the first time on Don Kirshner's show. Keith stood out because he was so capricious on the drums – and he was a volatile musician too, blowing up his drums live on stage while Townshend would be smashing his guitar to smithereens. Keith actually gave Pete permanent tinnitus during *The Smothers Brothers Comedy Hour*. He'd gotten a stagehand to put gunpowder in his kit but the guy used ten times the amount needed. During the finale of 'My Generation', Keith set off the charge and it was so intense that it singed Townshend's hair and pretty much cost him his hearing. For his part, Keith got a piece of cymbal stuck in his arm too.

Who else would think about blowing out their drum kit other than someone who is the Hendrix of the drums? In the same way that Hendrix set fire to his guitar, it's a way of saying, 'I'm burning everything down that you thought guitar was about, and I'm gonna take it from here.' Miles Davis made a similar statement with *Birth of the Cool*. Great musicians make statements that on the surface can be interpreted as just some crazy guy being crazy. No: Keith and Jimi took shots – shots at the system and the establishment. That's what the popular music we're talking about was doing; it was anti-establishment, it was rule-breaking and it was about redefining everything you thought you knew.

The Who were known for being crazy, but they also did some great songs. '5.15' and 'Love, Reign o'er Me' are epic productions that are album tracks – they're not even singles. The Who were a band on form and making amazing music. When Keith died from a drug that was supposed to help him get off booze, we lost one of the greatest drummers of all time.

*

There are many other people that belong in this chapter; some you'll find elsewhere in the book, others I didn't get the space to include. But from Miles Davis to Keith Moon, these iconoclasts of music have one thing in common: a Rock 'n' Roll heart and soul. These people were striving for perfection, not pounds. Musicians like James Brown could hear things that most ordinary ears couldn't comprehend; but when he played, we understood and appreciated every note. Being an 'icon' isn't about how many magazine covers you do: it's about taking an accepted idea of what is and making it what could be. What will be. By challenging the status quo and not just thinking outside of the box, but doing away with it altogether, it is James Brown and Frank Sinatra and Keith Moon who we have to thank for not just making great music, but for being really fucking awesome while they did it.

WALKING
THE
LINE

With a lot of the greats mentioned in this book, the same theme comes up time and again: they offer their emotions up on a plate to us, their listeners, with a rare, raw honesty.

When it comes to Rock 'n' Roll-style introspection, few can be said to match the late Johnny Cash. He was a crazy dude – like, a *really* crazy dude. There's the cliché that behind every good man... But that's incredibly true of some of our greatest musicians. June Carter Cash saved Johnny from himself.

Cash spent some time in the United States Air Force as a Morse code intercept and was the first US operator to pick up the news of Stalin's death in 1953. Shortly after that, he was honourably discharged. He'd started playing in a band in the Air Force, and as soon as he got out he started writing songs because I guess he had a need – like I did coming out of the United States Marine Corps – not to be normal. The best way to do that is to be a musician, so he started singing songs and he had a good voice for it, so he got picked up pretty quickly by people digging his stuff. And then he went off the deep end.

There's a great parody of Cash called *Walk Hard: The Dewey Cox Story* starring John C Reilly. It depicts Cash's crazy lifestyle and how he was doing pretty much everything that was offered to him. He was fortunate not to tip over the edge into the abyss, but then he met June. She knew who he was and what he was, and kind of schooled him a little bit. June was a star in her own right. She didn't need to marry Johnny and jump on his bandwagon. The Carter Sisters were doing their own thing. She wanted Johnny for Johnny and she saved his ass from a possible catastrophe, from being one more of our casualties of Rock.

One of the great things about Cash was that he went out and did really unusual things that no one else did. He went to San Quentin Prison, where he thought he'd find like-minded people. Those are some of the best performances he ever did. It's funny – if you listen to recordings like *Johnny Cash at San Quentin*, he talks to those guys like they're regular guys, and they loved that. 'You can yell all you want, but I've got the mic.'

In between songs he was always really good at talking to people. He was a born storyteller. Most people will know 'I Walk the Line' and 'Ring of Fire', but the dude made 96 albums. There are the Sixties and Seventies albums, but there are also records he did later on in life, like the cover of Nine Inch Nails' 'Hurt', so he became really popular with Trent Reznor fans. Or there's the *American Recordings* record, produced by Rick Rubin, where it was just him and a guitar, pretty much. He did a cover of Leonard Cohen's 'Bird on a Wire' on that album, and it's really great; it's Cash and a guitar and all of his life experience wrapped up into the one recording. He made a lot of great music, but if you just want to hear a man and a guitar, that's a really good example of how to put a mic in front of a guy and let him just do his thing.

Cash came in and out of fashion; he had such a long and interesting life. He hosted *The Johnny Cash Show* on US TV, did a *Columbo* episode where he played the bad guy, so he was an actor too, and he was good at it. It's a great *Columbo* to watch. Johnny Cash was an all-round kind of guy, before his time. If he had been on the scene ten or twenty years later we would have probably been more widely appreciative of his music. Everyone is like 'I love Johnny Cash' now, but there's a lot of stuff that people don't know about. He did a lot of religious things, especially towards the end of his life, lots of gospel, because he and June became quite religious. Musicians pretty much keep their religious beliefs quiet, but he was one of the guys screaming it from the rooftops. 'God saved me, I was a crazy man.' If it hadn't been for his wife, though, I think he would have lost it completely. But June and his religion gave Johnny the discipline he needed to keep going. And he lived a long and fruitful life. It was a sad thing to see him go.

In a lot of ways, Cash inspired the Punk movement. There's the iconic picture of him flipping everybody off. And he was like that – he was a rebel in the truest sense of the word and he encompassed a lot of the Rock-star mentality, but he was a Country singer. He had all the money and all the drugs and all the girls that he could handle, and from what I understand, he went through them as much as he could! Until he got to the point where he met the right woman. Speaking from experience, when you meet the right woman, you try to fuck it up. But if she's determined enough and you smarten up quick enough, things can turn for the better for you. It was later in Cash's career when he met June. He was really, really big by that point, and he met her and then he plateaued, but he didn't drop. He found something to live for. A lot of times, you get to a certain age, as a musician, where you wonder if you should give up. We're so preoccupied with youth and we look at these young kids like, 'Oh, they're so stupid – if I were them...' Well, you're not, because you're older, and you understand life a little bit more; you have a little bit of wisdom. And when people of that age are still doing quality music that's commercially relevant, it's a rarity.

Cash was also more political than people gave him credit for. He was very outspoken, so he'd play at the prisons, he'd play at churches, he recognized the massacre of the Native Americans. He was a socially responsibly guy, and that reflected in his music. He wasn't afraid to tell people how he felt. He never really gave a fuck. If he believed in something and it mattered to him, he'd tell you about it. Because he didn't care if you were going to buy his record or not. He was doing OK.

That's what I find really disappointing with a lot of the bands that are out there now. They have a really decent following and they have a political view but they mask it. They might put a free-trade sticker on their piano to make them appear political, but in essence, they're not coming out and saying anything.

And no one looks around a record like they did when The Beatles put out *Abbey Road* and everyone thought Paul McCartney had passed away and it was a new Paul McCartney. (There's a Volkswagen Bug on the album cover with LMW 28-IF as its number plate, and they're walking across the zebra crossing. Paul McCartney is barefoot, which signifies someone who's dead. So there was international speculation that Paul McCartney had died and they'd replaced him.) But that was when the myths of popular music were steeped in all this mysticism, when Zeppelin and Black Sabbath were trying to do weird things and put messages in their music if you played them backwards. Musicians rarely seem to do that any more – create intrigue and mystery and infuse subversive messages in their music. It's a shame, because that made it all so much more fun.

If you really want to know Johnny Cash, listen to 'Boy Named Sue' and just listen to the way he plays it. It was on *At San Quentin* and the way it goes over with the crowd... That right there is exactly what Johnny Cash did to people. He elicited a really personal message from himself and became personal to the people he was playing it to. As I've said, Johnny's life, in many ways, was saved by his wife, and so I guess we have June to thank too – without her, the lineage of socially conscious music would be severely lacking. And without Johnny Cash, who knows what line we might be walking today.

*

A HAUNTING REFRAIN

Communicating personal emotions was all part and parcel of singer Nico's allure. Aside from being one of the founding members of what we now call Indie music, Nico pretty much set the template for the Goth girl. If you listen to that record, *The Velvet Underground & Nico*, it's incredible; it has every nuance that we consider to be Indie nowadays.

They had John Cale on viola, they had Maureen 'Moe' Tucker on drums, and they had Lou Reed, the sexually ambiguous tortured soul. And then there was Nico in the role of chanteuse, with her Indie-girl-sounding voice and being all depressed and insular and insecure. She was a pre-Goth Goth! As a band, those guys were really honest with all the problems they were going through. They were singing their own Blues. They were talking about waiting for the man, the dealer: 'I'm sick.' There was poetry and anguish and torment, the cornerstones of all great Indie music. Reed wrote 'Sweet Jane', probably one of the coolest love songs ever, with the riff everyone now knows. I learnt that song early on. They were so influential as a collective that Brian Eno was quoted as saying that their debut might only have sold 30,000 copies in its early years, but 'everyone who bought one of those 30,000 copies started a band'.

Nico was only lead vocal on three songs on that record, so it's a pretty ballsy thing to say: 'I'll be in the band, but I want my own billing.' Particularly when, to all intents and purposes at that time, you're a nobody. But *The Velvet Underground & Nico* is how it ran. She was so contrary and I liked that about her personality. And she was a great songwriter too. When she did her fourth solo album, *The End...*, she took it to levels a Goth could only dream of reaching. You thought The Doors did a dark version of 'The End'; her cover of their record takes it to a whole new level of doom and gloom. It's chilling. The album was produced by John Cale and he throws his haunting piano on there, and then you have Brian Eno playing some of the most menacing synth you've heard. She has this one track called 'You Forgot to Answer', which is about unsuccessfully trying to reach her ex-lover, Jim Morrison, on the phone – only to discover later that he'd died.

It was clear Nico had talent from early on. She was German and had grown up in Berlin, been a model and stumbled to New York during the Sixties. There she met Brian Jones, who recorded her first single, with Jimmy Page producing the B-side. Those are some pretty serious co-signs to have. Jones introduced Nico to Warhol and that's when she appeared in films of his, like *Chelsea Girls*, before he made her part of The Velvet Underground.

Warhol's creative and chaotic involvement with The Velvet Underground saw the birth of different artists from different mediums sharing common ground. He quit painting to manage and produce the then-upcoming New York band. In New York City, these guys were all socializing together. Manhattan's not a big place; there were like ten places where people would hang out back then. They drank, maybe did some drugs, got creative. Pop art and Pop music went hand in hand. Later on, Warhol would do the artwork for *Sticky Fingers* for The Stones, but his banana for the Underground cover is the best Freudian imagery ever. That's how you make an iconic album cover and create an iconic band. That's what other Rock 'n' Roll albums aspire to. Art and music still go hand in hand nowadays, with every rapper and his dog bragging about how many Banksys they own. After Warhol and The Underground, you had Madonna and Basquiat, you'd see The Clash with all of the graffiti artists. Strummer wrote 'Futura 2000' with his buddy Futura, one of the most important graffiti artists of all time.

The Velvet Underground and Warhol were very concerned with

the visuals that went with the music. Warhol did lots of videos and films with them, creating one of the first multimedia projects, really; they'd have The Underground performing with a film playing behind them and strobes, and the Exploding Plastic Inevitable was born. The first performance was in front of 1,000 people at the Dom, a one-time Polish community centre on St Mark's Place in Manhattan, in 1966. Strobe lights flashed as the band played at full volume. Gerard Malanga pretended to inject himself with heroin on stage while Brigid Polke wandered through the crowd, injecting her friends with amphetamines. Presiding over it all from a balcony was Warhol, projecting silent films on a wall behind the band. 'We all knew something revolutionary was happening; we just felt it. Things couldn't look this strange and new without boundaries being broken,' said Warhol at the time. There was Nico, at the front of the stage, ethereal and still, singing simply in all her Indie-girl glory.

Warhol and Nico and The Velvet Underground were really into each other; you felt like they had a good, healthy respect for what each other was doing. Nico didn't stay with The Underground for ever, but her bandmates worked on many of her subsequent solo albums, joining the likes of Bob Dylan and Jackson Browne. Later on, her then-boyfriend Jim Morrison would encourage Nico to write her own songs – which she did. She wasn't just some pretty face, an ingénue or a muse brought in to look good and sing nice. Nico was a great talent who inspired people like Siouxsie and the Banshees, Patti Smith, Morrissey and Elliott Smith. Björk used to open her show with 'Le Petit Chevalier'. The Cult wrote 'Nico', while Marianne Faithfull wrote 'Song for Nico'.

If you're hanging with Lou Reed, you must have some clout. We needed Nico. She allowed women in music to get really, really dark. She gave those people a voice. What she did, people had maybe done before – say, Lady Day and 'Strange Fruit' – but she was at the forefront of so many cutting-edge things at the same time. Indie, Goth. Multimedia. Art. Music.

Nico partied with the best of them. She went pretty hard on the drugs, but (just about) lived to tell the tale. She died in 1988 at the age of 49, having recently given up heroin. Determined to live healthier, she had taken up cycling and healthy eating; ironically, on holiday in Ibiza with her son, she suffered a heart attack while riding a bike, hitting her head as she fell. A local cab driver found her and took her to hospital where she was misdiagnosed with heat exhaustion. X-rays later revealed she had died of a severe cerebral haemorrhage. But her influence and contributions are still celebrated. In 2013, John Cale organized a tribute to Nico at the Brooklyn Academy of Music; performers included Joan As Police Woman, Alison Mosshart, Peaches and Kim Gordon. She was a complex woman, but it seems fair to say that she and her music were all the more powerful for it.

*

MAKING A STAND

Like I said at the start of this chapter, so many of the greats had that unusual ability to communicate the depths of their soul to us with an immediacy that's almost shocking. One of the most thought-provoking artists in that respect, for me, is Joe Strummer. As a kid, Joe Strummer was my John Lennon, my James Brown, my Frank Sinatra. He was the guy who made me see beyond my neighbourhood. He offered me a worldly perspective and made it OK to enjoy and play different kinds of music. The Clash was highly influenced by Hip-Hop and Reggae and Rock. Mick Jones was a big fan of David Bowie and Queen. The band also had a background in the Blues, and they weren't afraid to mix that all together. That was something that influenced me a lot when we set up the Criminals; we weren't afraid to fuck around with any sound as long as we thought it was good.

That was the ethos of Punk Rock: to snub authority and to tell the truth when nobody else would. The Clash were anti-establishment, and they were also anti-big business. Although they were signed to a major label, they still spoke their minds. In the Seventies, that was encouraged, especially within the forum of Punk Rock. The Sex Pistols did it, Stiff Little Fingers did it really well, but The Clash did it better! And they pulled a lot of shit on their label; they would press discs without telling executives. Or they would surrender royalties because they wanted to release a three-disc album that the label had refused to finance. Their balls were always on the line.

They were such diverse personalities in The Clash and they brought out the best in each other. There were two singers in that band, and you could always tell if it was a Joe Strummer song or if it was a Mick Jones song. 'Lost in the Supermarket' is obviously a Mick song, and 'Clash City Rockers' is obviously a Joe song. 'London Calling' is also obviously a Joe song – he's telling his story about the Thatcher era and the economy

Ma Rainey, the woman who delivered unto us the Blues. She was the first recognized professional Blues performer and drove the recording explosion of the 1920s

Despite dying a well-off woman, Bessie Smith was buried in an unmarked grave thanks to her ex-husband preventing attempts to provide for a headstone. In 1970, Janis Joplin and Smith's former housekeeper, Juanita Green, jointly funded a tombstone for the legendary singer.

THE GREATEST BLUES SINGER IN THE WORLD WILL NEVER STOP SINGING BESSIE SMITH 1895 — 1937

Robert Johnson was a guitar player like no other. Keith Richards said of him: 'Want to know how good the blues can get? Well, this is it.'

When Billie Holiday sang, her soul shone through all that pain and addiction.
Something about Billie just stood out more than those around her.

Frank Sinatra, our inaugural Rock God, was charged with seduction aged 23 for having sex with a single woman 'of good repute'. The charges were dropped when the woman in question turned out to be married, but his mugshot remains an iconic image.

Ruth Brown was one of the first instances of any musician taking the reigns of her career and understanding the business side of it. That was a

Muddy Waters's 'Electric Mud' is such a definitive Blues record, that if you don't have 'Electric Mud' in your record collection, you don't have a record

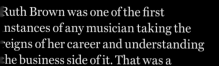

As a black Jewish man married to a white woman, Sammy Davis Jr got it from all sides. But he used his fame to break boundaries in so many ways; he was the first ever black man to stay overnight, as a guest of President Nixon, in the White House.

Miles Dewey Davis III took great intellectual joy in disrupting the rigid ideologies of what he'd been taught as a child prodigy in Illinois. He tore up the rulebook, and with such style.

Race relations of the time gave gasoline to these engines of artistic endeavour. To be so openly political was a huge risk for successful crossover artists, but because of people like Sam Cooke, a change finally did come.

Birth of the Cool really brought Miles Davis into mainstream consciousness – it showcased this new style of Jazz and had everyone following in its footsteps.

The late, great James Brown helped shape our notions of Rock 'N' Roll behaviour. He was pretty wild: car chases, drugs, messing with women – but people still loved him;

A natural on the piano, Nina Simone learned to play by ear at three years old, and later won a scholarship to the Juilliard School. Pictured here talking to fellow legend Otis Redding at the Regency Hyatt Hotel, Atlanta, Georgia, for a convention.

There's a cliché that behind every good man... But that's true of some of our greatest musicians. June Carter saved Johnny Cash from being a crazy person. She was a star in her own right, she didn't need to marry Johnny and jump on his bandwagon.

being shit and how everybody was pissed off. He really captured the mood of a nation: he was never shy about making a political statement.

Joe lived for trying to make people think. There's nothing better than music for that, when it's done as well as The Clash did it. Their music would be something you could listen to – the sound would hit you and the sentiment would hook you. Whether or not you agreed with Strummer's politics, you knew where he stood, and if you stood with him you felt empowered that there was somebody out there who had your point of view and was a humanist rather than a capitalist. A lot of times people capitalize on their fame for their own benefit, and they don't use it to help people that aren't as fortunate. You would hope that people would take cues from the men and women who went before them. I was doing that when I was making my music – taking cues from artists like The Clash and Marvin Gaye and people who told stories about the human condition. About how we all live our lives on this little rock three stones from the big old burning sun. Everything's so tenuous, but we always try to make it seem like everything is going to be OK.

There's an old building in Somerset, near my home, with this sign by artist Martin Creed saying, 'Everything is going to be alright' in neon lights on the side of it. It looks like a church that actually says it like it is. I think people want to believe that everything is going to be OK, that nothing is going to happen to them, but they have to accept their social responsibility, and that was backed up a lot by the music that we listened to in those days. It mirrored society.

A British band could express how their lives were in England, and make it relatable around the world to people like myself. It transcended the fact that they were making great music. Listen to their triple album, *Sandinista!*, from 1980. Sandinista is a word that came from Nicaragua, meaning either communist freedom fighter or terrorist, depending on what side of the government you were on back then. The Clash had a reason for everything; they never flippantly made a song or an album. Even their love songs are *real* love songs. They're about how real people deal with each other when they're in love. Like 'Train in Vain' – it's like 'Stand By Me' but done in a modern way. It shows how there are a lot of different things that happen in a relationship that are fuelled by external forces: they don't have a job, they don't have a house... Now a lot of artists like to sing/write about having and spending huge amounts of money. Being a well-rounded human being isn't as coveted as being a millionaire – like money is going to solve everybody's problems. And that only came from musicians making so much money – suddenly everybody desired to live that lifestyle.

In the beginnings of Hip-Hop the artists weren't rich – they were dressing like cowboys with leather pants up in the Bronx, looking like weirdos, like the New York Dolls, almost. It was so anti the neighbourhood; they were so different, and so brilliant. And then it started to become all about money and hoes and cars and blunts and asses. There's still great Hip-Hop out there, but because it's not regarded as commercially viable you rarely get to hear the artists who are speaking meaningfully about political and social issues.

I was looking at the first Clash record the other day, and it reminded me exactly why I liked the band. Before I even put the record on, I knew that these three guys were really fucking cool. They looked like they had something to say. They were wearing weird stuff and had patches on their sleeves. You could just see that Joe Strummer was a revolutionary dude. After he left The Clash he formed The Mescaleros, he released 'Johnny Appleseed', a song that people really slept on. There's a line that goes, 'If you're after getting the honey, hey/Then you don't go killing all the bees', which is a metaphor for a lot of things. It could be taken literally – which was pretty prescient considering the current bee crisis – but it could be looked at in many different ways. That's one of the things that I think people don't do nowadays. When you take the time to figure out double entendres and metaphors, people can tell that you really mean what you're singing about. It's easy for people nowadays to go on *The X Factor* or *The Voice* or *Britain's Got Talent* – they're talent shows for one-dimensional thinking. We want to know how hard they had it – one guy's a taxi driver, and he can sing like Pavarotti, but he's not going to win because he's old. We'll get the pretty young kid who looks like he could be a star, and we just pump him with catchy songs to put on his record. It's just a whole different mindset to people like Joe Strummer. When he died, a whole bunch of hope died with him.

I was a friend of his, and he was a friend of mine, and that was an unbelievable experience, because I wanted to be like him: to be a family man, to speak my mind, to try not to be an asshole. Anybody who came up to Joe at any point in the day, he'd take time out for. He said to me one time, 'If I make it possible for someone to change their life in some way, I've done my job.' He never claimed to be a prophet; he was a very humble man. And that was something that I wanted to emulate. I don't go to parties, I don't hang out with rich people and famous people, you don't see me in the back of *Grazia*. I have nothing in common with those people. I've got more in common with the guy from Brooklyn who plays guitar in a Funk band than I do with Kate Moss. I mean, I've met Kate Moss and she seems like a really nice lady, but I've got nothing in common with her. That's not why I got into music.

The Criminals and I were friends with Joe from about '97 till his death. Every time he'd come to New York he'd come to our studio. He was doing a bunch of shows in New York at one point, and we were recording, so he'd come by the studio and we'd talk about everything. He'd listen to our music and he'd say, 'You're getting there, man. Hear that? That makes you feel something right there.' He was never critical and he didn't tell us what we should change; he was always very encouraging.

Joe knew how I felt about him. When he first came into our dressing room at T in the Park, I was sitting in my underwear. I jumped up like, 'Joe mothafuckin' Strummer!' He goes, 'That's not my middle name!' Out of all the musicians I've met, Joe Strummer made the most lasting impression. He walked into our dressing room and, although they say you should never meet your idols, in Joe's case, it was the best thing that ever happened to me as a musician.

After meeting him at T in the Park, we hung out all day and then I saw him later on that year when he was in New York. We had friends in common – for instance the guy who art directed our first three records was good friends with him – so we'd all hang out, and that's how I got to meet Mick Jones when I moved to London. Joe was one of those guys who always had good people around him, and protective people, because they knew he was such a good guy. He would be able to talk people off ledges all the time. And he was one of the more giving human beings I've ever met – he was always really positive about everything. He always made you feel as though you were in the centre of some real upbeat, fun shit. A good friend of mine, the photographer Bob Gruen, who was a good friend of Joe's as well, always told me that when you went out with Joe, you had to remember to bring your sunglasses. I didn't understand until one time I walked outside with Joe. It was 8.30am and we were in midtown Manhattan, having been in some Irish bar lock-in. You kind of struggle with the sunshine at points like that, you know?

The last time I saw Joe was about six months before he died. He was in New York playing some gigs. He didn't look sick. He was still enthusiastic about what he was doing – at that time it was a week-long residency at this place in Brooklyn that held about a thousand people. He came and hung out with us at our studio and he never appeared weak or unwell.

I heard Joe had died when my buddy Dr Revolt called me up. He's a graffiti writer – he's in the film *Wild Style* – and he painted that mural of Joe at 7th Street and Avenue A. New York loved Joe as much as – if not more than – Joe loved New York. Apparently he'd been out walking his dog, and he came back and he just sat down and died.

I've got a picture of him right on my wall. Every once in a while I'll play him something and his expression will change slightly. I think that's in my mind and it's good that it's in my mind. Because Joe Strummer is still in my soul.

You get artists like Johnny Cash, Nico and Joe Strummer, who came on the scene at different times, but you can see a direct line. They did what they wanted, said what they wanted, lived the way they wanted, and made a place for themselves in the world of music that isn't going away. People are not going to forget The Clash and they're not going to forget Johnny Cash – that's what makes these great musicians so great. Without Nico we might never have had Goth. These guys did something so unique and singular and unto themselves, and very personal – they wore their hearts on their sleeves. And that's not something you get any more. That's why I think Johnny Cash, Nico and Joe Strummer were cut from the same cloth in a lot of ways – they were from different parts of the world, they had different upbringings, they had different musical styles, but they wanted to do something with their music that was beyond merely recreational listening. And I think that goes for a lot of the greats.

OUT
ON A HIGH

Jamie Foxx said it best when he said white people don't know the limits. They don't know about the edge. 'White people party to the edge of death,' he said during his 2002 stand-up *I Might Need Security*. 'Hey, there's the edge of death right there. There it is. Give me the cocaine, give me the GHB.' Let's face it, everyone has the capacity to go too far, no matter their race, creed or colour... And Rock 'n' Rollers have that in them more than anyone.

No one was guaranteed a tomorrow in Rock 'n' Roll if they were truly Rock 'n' Roll about it. And they didn't want that guarantee; that's why a lot of our favourite musicians lived every day like it was their last – because it very well might have been. Super-creative guys like Jimi Hendrix were trying to get to the next level. They wanted to reach a certain level of consciousness and they thought that the drugs bought them closer to it. Jim Morrison with the peyote and all of his weird poetry. The rumours of Hendrix having his headband lined with blotter. It's safe to assume John, Paul, Ringo and George took a few hits while recording *Sgt Pepper's*. That album could only be made on acid, right? By experimenting with hallucinogens, The Beatles made a 20th-century musical masterpiece that changed everybody's perception of how music was recorded. They revealed that songwriting could be made so simplistically beautiful – yet with all of this crazy psychedelic instrumentation. That record reached new heights, and perhaps in some ways encouraged other artists to aim higher. The next level was there and they could get there too if they wanted to.

But then, of course, drugs get a hold, and in a lot of cases the person ends up an addict; that's the sad part of it. Some people were predisposed to take it a little too far, but perhaps they would have taken it too far anyway. Taken *anything* too far.

In the exploration of the abyss, we lost a lot of talent. Some guys were looking for just too much information. Hendrix was a sponge for knowledge and experience and trying to achieve wisdom. Maybe it sounds hippy, but the drugs did move people in certain directions that were more creative. The more you take, the closer you get to the abyss, and some of them fell right in. Janis and Jimi are so missed because they made incredible music while surfing that wave; we lost the possibility of more when they went under. Who (if the stories are true) puts blotter acid in their headband and then puts it on their head so that the acid soaks into the bloodstream? A Rock 'n' Roller, that's who – a Rock 'n' Roll guitar player at Woodstock playing 'The Star-Spangled Banner', looking for the next level. They were explorers and it was uncharted ground.

Music and drugs have, historically, often gone hand in hand. I'm not saying everybody who listens to, or makes, music takes drugs (and certainly not that they should), but a lot of musicians who make popular music take drugs because it's part of the lifestyle in a lot of ways. It distances you from reality – and for some people that's where they feel they need to be if they're going to be creative. But it's dancing with danger: Hendrix and Jim Morrison, Amy Winehouse and Keith Moon, Shannon Hoon and Johnny Thunders – I mean, these guys knew the risks. Why did Johnny Thunders start taking all those drugs? He knew what was going to happen; he'd seen drugs take away so many of our greats. But I guess some people stop caring – or want to push as close to the edge as they can.

Music emancipated people who were trying to push boundaries with sound and expanding their minds through substances. The sexing came into it, too, particularly in the 'Swinging Sixties', because women and men were attracted to each other and inhibitions were lost, and the attraction was more easily acted upon. There was a freedom to it too.

That idea encapsulated Rock 'n' Roll for me as a kid; whatever you're going to do, do it to the upmost of your ability – be it rocking, drugging or sexing. And that's what this book is about. Some of these guys and women were doing it to the point of addiction. Ray Charles was an addict for years of his musical career. But he was a functioning one – because he was blind and had to wear sunglasses the whole time, no one could tell when his eyes were pinned! But that's one of the things that defines Rock 'n' Roll. 'Give me something.' 'What do you want?' 'Whatever you got.' It's the raw nerve. It's like dancing on the edge of the flat world, knowing that at any moment a gust of wind could knock you the fuck over, but you don't give a fuck because you're living something that no one else really lives. The second-best job in life is musician. The first is astronaut, but you can't take drugs. So... there you go, I'm out!

In my dictionary, Rock 'n' Roll would be this: the playing of music loudly, the living of life proudly, the acceptance of opportunities gladly, and... 'Can I have one more, please?'

I was 27 years old when I got signed to my deal. I was a grown man. I'd been in the Marines. I was older and I saw all these young kids in other bands going off the rails because it was the first time they had had access to sex and drugs on that scale, and they were also young enough to get up the next day and play a show. I had to take it easy because I knew I was 27 and if I went out and did eight grams of coke and drank a bottle of whisky, I couldn't get up the next day without crying. So I always kept it back a little. I've had moments where I can relate, but nothing to the extent of a lot of those guys.

In the early days of the Criminals, I tried really hard to be sex and drugs and Rock 'n' Roll; I had the supermodels and the actresses, but I didn't really do that many hard drugs; I was more of a weed man. I wasn't really a drinker either; I'd have champagne backstage, but that was for the girls. The band would all have a couple of beers each. Completely tame if you consider that, before us, people were doing heroin and freebasing and smoking coke! Rick James would hold people hostage in his house and burn them with crack pipes. There was some serious craziness going on, but there was also a fun-loving aspect to being Rock 'n' Roll in those days. When Keith Moon left the handbrake off that Rolls-Royce and it rolled into the pool, he knew he could buy another one tomorrow. It was no big deal. It was like buying a pack of cigarettes to him. That's how he rolled. Chuck Berry would be like, 'Rent me a Caddy at the airport. When I get to the gig, you rent me a Fender Twin and a Gibson ES-335, you get a band that knows all my songs, in any key. I show up, you give me a suitcase full of money, I lock it into the Caddy, I hold the keys in my pocket, I go on stage, I play the gig and I leave. And I keep the guitar.'

From my time around musicians, I've figured out one thing: we're all looking to fill a hole. A void. An emptiness within us. Sure, everyone has a hole to fill but it feels like, for musicians and actors and painters, that hole's a little bit bigger. I partied hard for a while, but ultimately I filled my hole with love, as corny as I know that sounds. My wife and my son. But a lot of people chose – or choose – drugs.

I knew that music would do it for me back in junior high school. I was in assembly and I just happened to be in the front row. There was this guy, Adam Rafferty, who was the cool kid of the school because he played guitar. He and his band came out and started playing 'Jumpin' Jack Flash'. Every hair on my prepubescent body stood on end. I knew right then that I wanted to do *that*. To be able to do what he was doing, something that seemed so totally outside of myself – that was what I wanted to do too. It's a question I ask a lot of people when I interview them on my show: why music?

There are some musicians who were so good at playing an instrument that they almost lost themselves in it, and that usually had something to do with them altering their own reality, chemically. They drank a lot, or did other drugs, to change themselves. If you can play or sing as good as the legends we're talking about do and did, then you're always going to want to take it to the next level and be the better artist. You always want to write a song that's better than the last.

The boredom factor plays a big part in the role of drugs and booze in Rock 'n' Roll. The work ethic involved in trying to be a good musician takes its toll. You do a gig, then you go to a party, you push on through, you get on the tour bus the next morning to do to the next town or city. You've had an hour or two hours' sleep; what are you gonna do the next night? You're tired and hungover, so you're gonna start drinking the minute you get to soundcheck. Unless you have self-discipline – and there's no externally imposed discipline being a musician, other than learning a craft.

Could Rock 'n' Roll exist in the same way without the influence of drugs? Possibly not. Who's to say. It's certainly a part of the formula. Sex + Drugs + Rock + Roll. Ian Dury said it and I'm inclined to agree. Perhaps kids today think they invented drugs, with their ketamine and their 'shrooms – but, as we all know, drugs ain't nothing new. Drugs and music have gone hand in hand since the days of Blues and its hooch and weed and pharmaceutical cocaine. Then you had marijuana and Jazz. Acid, amphetamines, heroin and cocaine during the Rock 'n' Roll years. Crack blighted the black community and became a big part of Hip-Hop's narrative in the Eighties, as rappers relayed the devastation that the drug wreaked on communities. Ecstasy got its big break during the rave years, and now horse tranquillizer is the drug of choice for Electronic Dance Music kids. What would music be without the presence of drugs? It's impossible to say, but it's hard to imagine Rock, House, Disco or Jazz without the input of pharmaceuticals of some form or other.

When music takes you to another place – whether that's through a drug or a natural high – it's something else. At the risk of sounding boastful, some of my music has taken me to a different place: I think it has to, otherwise what's the point? There are still moments on some of our earlier Criminals records where I listen and wonder how the hell we came up with a certain sound or phrase or moment.

But for the likes of Hendrix and Baby Huey, they got to a point where they were tired of all the cool things they were doing. They wanted to make even cooler things happen. They hadn't heard what they wanted to hear in their heads yet, and the drugs induced the feeling of getting towards that point. There was always a desire for more, for better, for greater, and a willingness to do whatever it took to get there.

These people have a mentality that is driven by something in their superego that makes them want to take things to the next level in what they do with their lives. Jim Morrison lived in a way that certain people thought unorthodox. Jim got arrested six times for crazy stuff like vagrancy and petty larceny after he stole a cop's helmet and umbrella. He got so drunk and obnoxious on a plane one time, going to see The Stones play, that he was arrested for interference with the flight of an aircraft. He'd take his pants down at shows and get arrested for that. Jim Morrison loved to push life to the limits and he ultimately paid the price with an early death – at the age of 27, of course.

Keith Richards, as a caveat to this chapter, is one in a million. The myth is that he's made of stone and nothing can kill him. Then you read his book, *Life*, and understand a little bit more about the man and how he wasn't as bad for as long as everybody thinks. But Keith left even

Gram Parsons in the dust. If you party with Keith, you'd better watch yourself. Everybody knows he's a hellraiser with super-human resilience so partying with him will be wild. Just watch Johnny Depp do that Captain Sparrow thing; that's how we look at Keith, like a caricature. But Keith has been on the one every time I've seen him play or watched videos of him; he has always slayed. And when you meet the man, you realize he's really a straight guy. He's clear and intelligent. He might still get high once in a while, but that's what you do if you're Keith Richards.

*

GOD BLESS THE CHILD

Billie Holiday set the template for the tortured singer fighting a losing battle with drugs. She was the archetype for the wayward woman of music. There were so many after her – Mama Cass, Janis Joplin, Amy Winehouse – and the drugs eventually swallowed them whole too, in one way or another. With Billie, there were times you could hear so acutely that she was attempting to dull the pain of that crazy, tumultuous life of hers, in any way she could. But when she sang, her soul shone through all that pain and the addiction and the abusive upbringing. That was the unique thing about Billie Holiday: she pushed the boundaries in her personal life and that could be heard in her music. There were other musicians of her time who had similar struggles, but Billie was held in such great esteem because she was such an incredible singer who had a particularly vulnerable, raw delivery. Something about her just stood out that little bit more than those around her.

Details of Billie's upbringing can be sketchy, but whatever way you look at it she had a really rough childhood. *Really* rough. This kid went through everything you can imagine, and then some. Eleanora Fagan was born in Philadelphia – or Baltimore, according to some sources – in 1915, to a teenage mother said to be as young as 13. Her father, 15 at the time of Billie's birth, was a successful Jazz musician called Clarence Holiday (though this is also sometimes disputed). As Billie was quoted as saying, 'You can't expect children to bring up children.' Her mother was away working a lot on the passenger railroads, trying to keep the family fed and together, so Billie was regularly put into the care of often-abusive relatives. She played truant a lot and, when she was nine, she was sent to the House of the Good Shepherd, a Catholic reform school. At the age of ten, she was sexually assaulted by a neighbour, but was sent back to the reformatory for 'seducing' her attacker. She turned to prostitution as a teen, for which she was arrested at 14. That's a hell of a lot of shit to go through before you've even turned into an adult. It was, in a horrible twist of fate, through selling her body that Billie finally found some sort of salvation. She would listen to Jazz on the brothel's phonograph and she taught herself the standards, mimicking the voices of folks like Ma Rainey. A couple of years later, she picked up and headed to New York, where she got a job as a singer in a speakeasy called Jerry's Log Cabin in Harlem.

Here's what she said of getting her first gig at around the age of 16. The story was published in *Big Star Fallin' Mama* by Hettie Jones, in 1974:

One day we were so hungry we could barely breathe. I started out the door. It was cold as all-hell and I walked from 145th to 133rd… going in every joint trying to find work... I stopped in the Log Cabin Club run by Jerry Preston... told him I was a dancer. He said to dance. I tried it. He said I stunk. I told him I could sing. He said sing. Over in the corner was an old guy playing the piano. He struck 'Trav'lin'' on and I sang. The customers stopped drinking. They turned around and watched. The pianist... swung into 'Body and Soul'. Jeez, you should have seen those people – all of them started crying. Preston came over, shook his head and said, 'Kid, you win'.

She must have really had something, even then.

Billie really went through it as a kid, so as a young adult her voice was infused with all of that pain that she carried with her. She fused the sentiment of all those before her – the Blues and Jazz men and women – and created something new but also familiar and fragile. Although she was completely untrained and couldn't read music, you couldn't deny the power of Billie's performance. Her vocal immediately clicked with your brain because there was no pretence.

Later in *Big Star Fallin' Mama*, she's quoted as saying that she thought of her voice more as a musical instrument. 'I don't think I'm singing. I feel like I'm playing a horn. What comes out is how I feel.' Bessie Smith and her 'big sound' and Louis Armstrong and the emotion he infused into his music were her two big inspirations.

By this point, she was known as Billie Holiday – she took her stage name from the film star Billie Dove, and her surname from her father. The way Holiday phrased things and improvised was magical. She had such a way with phrasing; check out her version of George Gershwin's 'Summertime'. You can hear that magic with Janis Joplin's version of the old standard, and John Coltrane's version of it. All the greats who died young picked that song to sing, perhaps because it touched a lot of religious and cerebral overtones. It really brings out the melancholy in a person. But Billie managed to create something just that little bit different from anybody else singing the exact same song – I think because she took a lot more chances with opening up her heart. When you do that, there's a very good chance that people are going to sling arrows at it. And, in Billie Holiday's case, they did just that.

Artists are very sensitive and empathic people; they need to be, to be able to pick up on what's going on with everybody else in the world. The reason that they're universally loved and respected is because they touch on something that's inside of everybody. It makes me wonder when we're going to see something or someone like Billie Holiday again. Because everything now seems so contrived, that it's almost as if someone is rolling out a carpet, and you know when and where the carpet is going to end. They've measured it. It's going to run its course and then that's that. I don't see One Direction being around in ten years. And if they are, we're all shit out of luck.

Billie's career spanned three decades. Once she started singing, her rise to success was pretty immediate; she hit the Harlem circuit and before long she was performing with Benny Goodman and then Duke Ellington. Saxophonist Lester Young nicknamed her 'Lady Day' in 1937 – the same year she joined Count Basie's band. Holiday had a bunch of trouble with many of the men in her life, but not Basie. He didn't have any designs on her; he let her do her thing. He looked at her as an equal and treated her as an artist, rather than as a singer for hire. He got on her side because of that. Being in Basie's band was the first time Billie got to experiment with music and really make a song her own. With Basie, she was around exemplary musicians who were really on the one. 'The cats would come in, somebody would hum a tune. Then someone else would play it over on the piano once or twice. Then someone would set up a riff [rhythmic pattern], a ba-deep, a ba-dop. Then Daddy Basie would two-finger it a little. And then things would start to happen,' she is quoted as having recounted in *Big Star Fallin' Mama*.

It was when she became the first black woman in Artie Shaw's all-white band that Billie became visibly politicized. She encountered plenty of racism while on tour with Shaw, especially down South where she was told she couldn't eat with the band or that she had to use a particular toilet. At one venue in Kentucky, a man made a racial slur against Holiday: justifiably enraged, she lashed out and had to be smuggled out for her own safety. Being from a city like Philly and living in Harlem, Billie wasn't used to segregation on this level. In '39, she began to sing the track 'Strange Fruit', written by Abel Meeropol, which talked about lynching. Though she said she was afraid to sing it for fear of retaliation, it became a regular in her sets and was a powerful closer. She said she sang it for her father, Clarence, who had died from a lung disorder after being refused hospital treatment because of the colour of his skin. Billie knew the trouble singing protest songs could bring her, but she did it anyway. She did it because she was a black American, and black Americans were being hanged from trees, or made to sit at the back of the bus; she felt an obligation as a human being and a black American to say something.

Billie had a number of affairs and marriages, but her greatest love was heroin. She was allegedly turned on to it by her first husband, Jimmy Monroe, and became addicted. The drugs really took hold of Holiday, who had already been going pretty hard with booze and weed. Once heroin and opium came into play, it ravaged her body pretty quickly. You can see from some of her live performances that she wasn't always quite there – especially later ones. That doesn't really happen much nowadays – you don't see people obviously wacked while they're playing – though I remember seeing that last concert that Amy did in Belgrade, which was heartbreaking to watch. You got the feeling with Amy – and Billie – that there was no one there to step in and help. Though she'd had a troubled upbringing, Billie was great friends with her mother, Sadie. Some say that when Sadie died, Billie lost the one person in her life that she could really trust to look out for her. Without Sadie's guidance, Billie was allowed to wither and die.

Abusive relationships didn't help – she later married another drug fiend, trumpeter Joe Guy, who fed her addiction to the point where she was jailed for eight months for possession of drugs. Her Cabaret Card was revoked, meaning she wasn't able to perform in clubs any more. Her voice weakened, she barely performed and she deteriorated fast. There were more arrests, more drugs, weight gain – this was a woman really fighting her demons, and losing. In the Fifties, broke, she wrote her autobiography *Lady Sings the Blues* with William Dufty – when questioned on the validity of certain claims in the memoir, she's said to have snapped, 'I've never read that book!' In 1959 she finally succumbed to heart and liver failure. The grip of addiction was so tight at that time that she was arrested for possession while on her deathbed and spent her last days being watched over by police officers.

The late, great Lena Horne summed up her friend pretty well in this 2008 interview from *Scoop USA*: 'Billie didn't lecture me – she didn't have to. Her whole life, the way she sang, made everything very plain. It was as if she were a living picture there for me to see something I had not seen clearly before. Her life was so tragic and so corrupted by other people – by white people and by her own people. There was no place for her to go, except finally, into that little private world of dope. She was just too sensitive to survive.'

Billie had lived an extraordinary life that made the lives of ordinary people that little bit better. 'Singing songs like "The Man I Love" or "Porgy" is no more work than sitting down and eating Chinese roast duck, and I love roast duck,' she wrote in her autobiography. 'I've lived songs like that.' The Lady no longer sings the Blues, but the Blues still weeps for the Lady.

*

400 POUNDS OF SOUL

Drugs took some of our greats before they even had the chance to be great. Not too many know and appreciate James Ramey, also known as Baby Huey. Some people will probably know 'Hard Times' but he remains pretty obscure. But if you see his album cover just once in your life, you'll remember it for ever because here's this big dude, six-three, with this huge Afro and a goatee and the album is emblazoned with the words *The Baby Huey Story: The Living Legend*. And then you find out he was dead before the record even came out. It's like *A Confederacy of Dunces* for the music world. *A Confederacy of Dunces* is this awesome novel by a guy called John Kennedy Toole, who committed suicide aged 31. After his death, his mother found the manuscript in his room and took it to a local college professor who took it to a literary agent and got it published pretty much immediately. It went on to win the Pulitzer Prize. Baby Huey might not have won any awards, before or after his death, but his talent is still felt in music to this day.

The story goes that it was Donny Hathaway who told Curtis Mayfield to check out this new band, Baby Huey & the Babysitters. Huey, from Indiana, had formed The Babysitters in Chicago in 1963. 'We played and sang our hearts out in small clubs. We weren't very good in the early days, but we worked hard to get the sound and effect and the show we wanted,' he told Minnesota's *Daily Journal* in 1969. 'I think the day of the big band is coming back. That's why we've got nine men and a big sound. We looked all over for the right guys and over the years we've put them together.'

Mayfield went to hear Huey and his band play at the Thumbs Up club in Chicago. Huey was this fucked-up, drugged-out, crazy man who had this *voice*. One minute he'd sound like Otis Redding, the next he's be screaming and howling and wailing. A prototype Prince in some ways, perhaps. He was also noted for inspiring rap; his bandmates remember him adding self-referential rhymes to his live shows, a style that would be replicated by Bronx kids in the late Seventies, years after Huey's death. You might not think you've heard his album, but you will know snatches of it from Hip-Hop: Ghostface Killah, The Roots and A Tribe Called Quest have all sampled or covered tracks from *Living Legend*. Baby Huey was a big influence on Hip-Hop; that's where I first heard about him, from Hip-Hop DJs, when someone passed me a cassette.

He was one of the most dynamic live performers ever. He would introduce himself on stage with the words, 'I'm Baby Huey and I'm four hundred pounds of Soul.' You can hear that quarter-ton of Soul on his live version of 'A Change is Gonna Come', which is on the *Living Legend* album. He does this spoken psychedelic break: 'About twenty years of very serious smokin' (smokin', smokin') ... a few trips (trips, trips), a little space odyssey once in a while...' He was pretty much saying, 'Here I am in outer space searching for new galaxies.' Unfortunately he died before the record came out and we didn't get a chance to thank him.

Baby Huey was going to be the next guy. A record he'd released the year of his death, 'Mighty, Mighty Children (Unite Yourself This Hour)', had sold some 200,000 copies. Pretty significant numbers, even for that time. He played at infamous clubs like Cheetah in New York, where one of the Rothschild family saw him play and told Baron de Rothschild about him. Baby Huey and the band were shipped out to Paris to play at the baron's daughter's debutante party. Things were in place for Baby Huey to become one of the greats.

And let's face it, Curtis Mayfield wasn't a guy to hang out with idiots; he saw not only an amazing musician but also a completely unique individual. Curtis wrote some tracks for *Living Legend* and put it out on Curtom Records, his own label – a posthumous release for Huey, who'd died of a heart attack after returning from a gig in Wisconsin. He was a heroin addict and a drinker too, and I guess when he hit 400 pounds, his heart just couldn't take any more. He died in a motel room in the south side of Chicago in 1970 at the age of 26. The guy, essentially, died to get that record out. He gave it his all and you can tell with that record, because every song has some magic in it.

*

FLYING HIGH

A lot of the myth around Hendrix and the drugs he took tends to overshadow the rest of him. He was a lot of things besides a Rock 'n' Roll casualty and the best guitar player that ever lived. James Marshall Hendrix was a soldier, a paratrooper; he was a commando. People forget that. He enlisted in the United States Army at the age of 19 and was in the 101st Airborne; that's a pretty badass uniform. You don't just walk into that. You have to jump out of a lot of planes and kick a lot of ass. He was honourably discharged a couple of years later, after breaking an ankle during a parachute jump.

There's also another story that I heard, about Jimi pretending to be gay. He could see what was happening in Vietnam and didn't want any part of that so he stuck his hand up and announced, 'Sorry, guys, I'm gay. I like men.' 'You can't be in the Army if you're gay, Jimmy.' 'Ah, shit, that's a shame. So long!' He didn't want to go to war, and he supported a lot of veterans' charities, but behind the scenes. There was a lot of social activism going on back then, but more privately; a lot of dudes used their influence and their money and didn't want the credit. We tend to remember figures like Jimi for choking to death on his own vomit. But this guy was so much more than that.

After the Army he became a session musician, playing guitar for the likes of Ike and Tina Turner and Sam Cooke. It was after playing in Little Richard's band that he formed his own – Jimmy James and the Blue Flames. The bassist from The Animals, Chas Chandler, later persuaded him to change the spelling of Jimmy to Jimi. It was through Chandler that Jimi first came to England; he agreed to meet Chandler, by then his manager, in London, partially on the promise that Chas would introduce him to Clapton. Legend has it Hendrix arrived at Heathrow with his pink hair curlers, some acne cream, a change of clothes and his guitar. Two days later, Jimi was jamming on stage with Clapton, Jack Bruce and Ginger Baker.

Jimi broke so much ground by looking at the guitar as an instrument of expression as opposed to something that just makes a sound. He lived through his guitar. You could hear it sing, you could hear it cry and you could hear it laugh. He even made it sound like a machine gun – he's talking about Vietnam during the live performance of 'Star-Spangled Banner', straight up. He would play it with his teeth, he'd play it behind his back – no one had ever seen shit like this before. Like James Brown, Hendrix was a showman, an entertainer, a progressive. He made all of the other guitar players of that day – Clapton, Beck, Page, The Beatles – even better. It was said that Jimi's friendship with, and influence on, Miles Davis is what drove Miles to forsake the old style of Jazz and led him to create atonal, batshit-crazy classics like *Bitches Brew*. Guys like

Miles looked at what Jimi was doing and knew they needed to bring it harder. All of those guys would go to Jimi's gigs and be aghast not just at how technically proficient he was, but also at what he was doing with the guitar. It was like taking a hammer and smashing it. It was something so deeply personal. You hear what he played and how he played it and you felt it. He was left-handed and apparently had hands that were twice the size of normal people's. His hands would be all over that guitar.

At an infamous performance in Monterey in 1967, Jimi set fire to the guitar. He'd been introduced on stage by Brian Jones, before playing blistering versions of 'Foxy Lady', 'The Wind Cries Mary' and 'Purple Haze'. At the end, he torched that motherfucker. *Rolling Stone* called it 'one of rock's most perfect moments'. The LA Times noted that he'd 'graduated from rumour to legend'. Hendrix himself said, 'I decided to destroy my guitar at the end of the song as a sacrifice. You sacrifice things you love. I love my guitar.'

His dad, James 'Al' Hendrix, who encouraged Jimi's talent, bought him his first acoustic guitar for $5 when Jimi was 15 years old. When he was 16, Al bought him his first electric guitar, a Supro Ozark 1560 S. By the mid-1960s he was playing Fenders, then Gibson Flying Vs and maybe a little Les Paul. But he was known for pretty much one guitar: the Fender Stratocaster, which he used on *Band of Gypsys*. Back then, they were making great guitars – this was the Sixties and Seventies, and you could buy a guitar off the shelf and it would be a really well-made 1957 Strat and you'd probably pay around $200. A '57 Strat could now cost you $50,000.

Jimi was one of those guys who come around once in a while and change things up – like Phil Lynott. I have to mention Phil Lynott here real quick. There are of course black people in Ireland, but back in the Sixties when he was a teenager, he must have had the roughest fucking life growing up there mixed-race. But he wrote the sweetest, most beautiful music. What Phil did with Thin Lizzy was incredible, not only musically but they were also breaking ground with racial barriers. He must have had to do that just by simply walking around; he was a big, bass-playing mixed-race dude. And because he was mixed-race, everybody had something to say; the black people had something to say, the white people had something to say. He lived in Dublin, in a city that was predominantly white and where racist attitudes still pervaded. He had to go through a lot as a kid, and we've already seen how going through stuff like that can affect the rest of your life. But the fact that he was able to put that aside and write the most beautiful love songs is amazing. He did a record called *Solo in Soho* – a great record. Mark Knopfler plays on it, Midge Ure's there, Huey Lewis plays harmonica. Like Jimi, you could tell there was so much love in that dude. You have to love something to really be good at it. You have to love playing the guitar or singing or writing lyrics. Lynott wrote such profound love songs.

Another guitar great who goes largely ignored is Rory Gallagher, another Irish player. I have a replica of a 1960 Strat of his; it's beautiful. It always seems that the guys who are best at playing instruments are the most troubled, the ones with the most demons. John Bonham and Keith Moon. Probably the two best drummers ever to pick up sticks.

They were fucking nuts. That's probably why they picked up drumsticks: so they could hit shit with them.

We lost a lot of these guys way before their time. Jimi's in the 'infamous' 27 Club – that long list of musicians who died three years short of 30. But experience in your life differs wildly. A 27-year-old Justin Timberlake is going to be very different to a 27-year-old Jimi Hendrix. One kid was groomed from the Mickey Mouse Club since he was twelve years old and the other was a guy from Seattle who joined the Army, like his dad before him, until he saw what was happening in Vietnam and became one of the greatest guitar players of all time. The things Jimi did – he actually channelled his soul through his instrument and very rarely do people do that.

Apparently he could be a mean son of a bitch when he was drunk or high, but you could tell Jimi was a good soul. He was a good-looking, charming guy and there was no pretence. I think Nirvana were the last band without pretence. They came out and they did what they did. They made videos because they fucking had to, so they made them as dark and weird as they possibly could. They were making great music. They were self-conscious but they weren't too self-aware. They were a three-piece, rocking it out. They were one of the last bands to do that properly.

Both Kurt and Jimi struggled with drugs. Jimi needed to go to the outer limits to be the man who he was. Some people are born with the predisposition to excess. It's almost like neither Jimi nor Kurt cared what happened to their bodies. If their art was better, that's what counted. If they wrote a better riff or hit a higher note or they could make that certain sound... It's about making the sound that they hear in their head, but they're trying to get it out and it's the hardest thing. It's frustrating. Frustration leads to people ingesting external influences, putting things into their bodies to try to make what's inside of them better.

You have to watch that Woodstock performance where Jimi had on the headband supposedly lined with strips of blotters; so when he sweated, the acid went into his head and straight into his bloodstream. Maybe that's why the United States national anthem sounded so fucking awesome when he played it that time. It's four minutes of insane psychedelia, and, man, does he make that guitar sing. People thought he was being deliberately unpatriotic playing 'The Star-Spangled Banner' in that way, but he played it because he was an American, a soldier, 101st Airborne Division, a badass. He was paying homage. He was actively paying tribute to a country that he loved and that he knew was better than it was. You don't see hatred in Jimi when he plays music – you see someone playing from the soul.

It's obvious: if you're hungry, you eat. So if you're a crazy Rock 'n' Roller and you're thinking to yourself, 'Well, I need to take it to the next limit', then maybe you wrap a band of hallucinogens round your head. Take Jim Morrison. He had no fear of death. It wasn't just about him. It was about writing some beautiful shit, right up there with T S Eliot and whoever. There was also ego, too. I mean, these guys and women, as nice as they were, had ego. We all, as humans, have a certain ego that is prevalent in what we do. There's ego involved in our lifestyles and how we interact with other people, and that's true when you're a musician, too. You know, Jimi Hendrix – nicest guy in the world, right? But he doesn't look like a guy you'd start messing around with.

If you were a jerk, he would probably handle himself adroitly just by verbalizing you into the ground. He wouldn't even have to hit you. The way he used his ego, he knew that he was a smart dude and he knew the dangers of taking all those crazy fucking drugs, but he thought that's what he needed to do to get to the next level. It's always about trying to get to the next level and changing the game. He already changed the game once with his debut album, *Are You Experienced*, so he tried to continually change the game with every record he put out. He was even more involved with the production of *Axis: Bold As Love*; he was in the studio for every twist of the knob. He recorded *Electric Ladyland* between London and New York. His third and final album was the first Hendrix record to go to number one. At the time of his death, Jimi was the world's highest-paid performer.

You can see when he's playing on *Band of Gypsys*, there was a sound coming that was getting a lot more Funk-infused. Who knows where they might have taken it next. He was hanging out with more of that Funk scene that was going on in the early West Coast, late Sixties/early Seventies sound like Tower of Power, Charles Wright & the Watts 103rd Street Rhythm Band, and Sly and the Family Stone. You could see them gathering together a percussion player and keyboard player – you could see Jimi trying to take it to somewhere that mixed elements of Rock with Funk, Sly and the Family Stone with a Hendrix twist. It would have been unreal. But that's all speculation because we'll never know. The poor bastard ended up with a girl that didn't know to turn him on his side, so he choked to death.

*

MIND, BODY & SOUL

Janis Joplin was so fragile and vulnerable – like many artists are, but with people like Janis and Billie you could really see and feel it. Artists like Janis had to go through so much pain and misery and they channelled that on stage. You hear it through a guitar amp. Sometimes you hear it through the PA of a vocal. And you hear it on a record. Otis Redding could sing the alphabet and he'd make your heart stop.

Hearing Janis sing was pure, unadulterated emotion. You heard her joy, you heard her pain, you heard her vulnerabilities. I imagine one of the few times she was really able to be herself was on stage singing. Everything came out, the joy and the pain. Aside from hearing it, you could taste it, you could smell it. Listening to Janis sing was a sensory overload. You hear Billie Holiday do 'Summertime' and then you hear Nina Simone do 'Summertime' and you hear Janis Joplin do 'Summertime'. These three women sang it in three completely different ways, but the emotion is there in all of their versions. It's awe-inspiring.

Holiday – alongside Lead Belly and Bessie Smith – were Joplin's greatest inspirations. She grew up in Port Arthur, Texas, during the Forties and said of the town, 'What's happening never happens there.' Given that she was an icon of counterculture, Joplin couldn't have come from a more square place: Port Arthur was an affluent city made rich by oil. It was reported throughout her career that her parents had disowned their hippy daughter, but her sister, Laura, later refuted those rumours. Janis was an outcast at school, though, called a 'pig', a 'creep' and a 'nigger lover' by her peers, who scorned the budding painter. She had wild hair and dated kids from the wrong side of the tracks. She was political, she read Ginsberg, she rejected segregation. 'They thought I was completely insane; they didn't like me,' she said in a 1969 interview in London. 'You know how small towns are; you're supposed to get married when you get out of high school. You're supposed to have a brood of children, and keep your mouth shut. And I didn't do any of those things.'

During high school, though, Janis found a group of fellow freaks, one of whom introduced her to the Blues. Soon she was soaking up Odetta and Big Mama Thornton. She would cross the river to Louisiana with her pals to visit bars where they could listen to the Blues. She just wasn't like other kids. Even when she was a little older and studying in Austin at the University of Texas, the campus paper ran a profile of the nineteen-year-old Joplin headlined 'She Who Dares to Be Different'. 'She goes barefooted when she feels like it, wears Levis to class because they're more comfortable, and carries her Autoharp with her everywhere she goes so that in case she gets the urge to break into song, it will be handy. Her name is Janis Joplin.' There was hostility too: she was voted 'Ugliest Man on Campus' by the frat boys. But it was while studying art at college that she released her first song, and she began singing in a bar called Threadgill's, where they paid her in beer. Through singing she found an escape. Quitting school, she packed her bags and headed to San Francisco.

Here Joplin delved into the Beat scene, known for Folk and amphetamines, and the path to addiction began. Speed became her drug; she lost huge amounts of weight, and was covered in needle marks. She decided to head back home and straighten herself out. She enrolled at college, got on with her parents, gave up singing, got engaged to her boyfriend, JP. Life was good. Or so it seemed. But then JP disappeared and it all fell to pieces. She turned to the thing she knew would make it all better: music.

Janis started gigging in Austin again, and picked up great reviews. Before long, she was back in California, fully aware of what that might mean. 'Mother and Dad,' she wrote in a letter to her parents around that time. 'With a great deal of trepidation, I bring the news. I'm in San Francisco. I understand your fears at my coming here & I must admit I share them... I love you so, I'm sorry.'

In the time she'd been away, beatniks and speed had gone – LSD and hippies were the new thing. She joined Big Brother and the Holding Company, and brought a real kick to the band. She stayed straight for a while, adamant that she would leave the band if drugs were bought around her. Inevitably, someone brought mescaline round, and though she initially freaked out, the need crept in.

Drugs eventually became her downfall, and she died, aged 27, just a couple of weeks before Jimi OD'd at the same fateful age. She was found in the Landmark Motor Hotel in Hollywood. The cause of death was an overdose of heroin, possibly compounded by alcohol.

*

By the time the artists mentioned in this chapter reached the end of their days, premature death seemed to be the only outcome. It's easy in retrospect to look at them and romanticize the idea of the tortured artist, whose art seems to lead them in a wild dance towards death. But in the end, as well as being phenomenal musicians, they were just people: people who had tendencies towards certain problems, who didn't manage to beat the odds. We're lucky we had them for as long as we did, and music would never have been the same without them.

FIGHT
THE
POWER

It is perhaps no small coincidence that so much great music came out of the Sixties, a decade of such political turmoil and public unrest. The international chaos caused by the two world wars may have become distant memories by then, but the US and UK still had plenty of fires raging at home and abroad, namely the demand for civil rights and the war in Vietnam. The Sixties produced some of the most powerful, moving, enduring music precisely *because* people were living in such dark, testing, fucked-up times within their own country and communities. There was no escape, and music became a form of both deliverance and declaration.

The inherent racism in America and Britain fuelled an abundance of music throughout the Fifties and Sixties. People started singing explicitly about the injustice they saw all around them. Until then, with some exceptions, protest songs tended to be veiled in innuendo and metaphor. Their messages were still heard, of course – if you knew what you were listening to, you knew. Protest songs have existed since people started putting words to music.

There were songs addressing the environment as far back as 1837, with 'Woodman, Spare That Tree'. Since the days of slavery and the spirituals, through the arrival of the Blues, music has reflected and rallied against what goes on in this crazy, fucked-up world. The incredibly moving 'Sometimes I Feel Like a Motherless Child', a spiritual from the 1870s, was about children being sold into slavery. The lyrics are so potent that everyone from Odetta to Ike and Tina Turner and Ghostface Killah has revisited it over the years. 'Oh, Freedom' and 'Go Down Moses' are two other great examples of spiritual standards that challenged oppression.

In 1911, activist Joe Hill stood up for the 'workingmen of all countries' with his song 'The Preacher and the Slave'. Blind Willie Johnson is said to have nearly started a riot at a New Orleans courthouse, performing 'If I Had My Way I'd Tear the Building Down'. Fats Waller's 1929 '(What Did I Do to Be So) Black and Blue' fast became a Jazz standard, while Lead Belly's 1939 hit 'The Bourgeois Blues' invoked the lines 'Home of the brave, Land of the Free, I don't want to be mistreated by no bourgeoisie'. The actor and singer Paul Robeson was an outspoken advocate of equal rights in the Thirties and Forties, and was so openly in support of pro-Soviet policies that he was investigated for 'Un-American Activities'. Like I said, people whose voices are suppressed have long found a way to channel it through music.

But the dam really burst with the advent of Nina Simone's 'Mississippi Goddam' and Sam Cooke's 'A Change is Gonna Come', both released in 1964 at a time of great civil rights activism inspired by Martin Luther King Jr and Malcolm X, among others. Adversity became the fuel for this music to emerge from a culture of hatred and anger; there was a renewed insistence that equality should be a given right in our constitution. It's impossible to think what music might be like now if musicians hadn't had all that crazy bullshit to react to and rally against.

When the Civil Rights Movement was in full swing, the majority of black and minority musicians were making music along those lines. There were very few who just closed their eyes to what was going on. Folk realized the strength to be found in numbers. If you love the music of Sam Cooke or Marvin Gaye and you hear them singing about something deep, it's going to affect your thinking. If you're a white person with an undecided mind as to what was going on, because you weren't politically aware or whatever, then maybe you too would be like, 'Yeah, this is bullshit. I'm not down with it.' If, when I was a kid, Van Halen had told me Coca-Cola was bad and I should probably drink Pepsi, I probably would have drunk Pepsi! Songs like Coltrane's 'Alabama' and the Staple Singers' 'Long Walk to DC' had a big part in helping the Civil Rights Movement because they were anthems that people could sing along to. Martin Luther King Jr knew he needed a soundtrack for his speeches and he knew that Jazz, Folk, R&B and Gospel would help radicalize and motivate America. That's something that's lacking in the charts, and, to an extent, in politics today. People lack backbone. They don't say what they feel for fear of backlash.

It wasn't just civil rights these guys were addressing: Bill Withers wrote a song called 'I Can't Write Left-Handed' (1973), which told the story of a veteran of the Vietnam War returning home disabled – sampled by Fatboy Slim on 'Demons' and covered memorably by John Legend and The Roots – and it is one of the most eloquent anti-war songs ever written. I play the live version recorded at Carnegie Hall on my show as much as I can. That song moved me to tears when I first heard it. I couldn't believe a person could create such emotion just by the way he was telling a story. It was done so perfectly and not self-consciously. Withers just told you a simple story but it was also a quiet call to revolution.

A lot of musicians and activists came together to try to effect change, and they should be hailed for that. They knew they could be facing personal risk from the many people who didn't agree with them, but they were on a path to making things better. There was nothing anyone was going to tell these people that would make them change their minds. It's a pretty fucking brave thing to do – to put out records like some of these guys did.

Music, compared to film or art, is particularly valuable in affecting public opinion when it comes to conscious thought. It's something that we've chosen as a society to invest in, to get behind, to create tribes and cultures around. Fine art, painting and sculpture are still seen as very exclusive and excluding in many ways. They're perceived as a privilege of the upper classes. But music is so universal and accessible. It can touch you if you're a learned person with a bunch of letters after your name, or if you're Joe Blow from Bensonhurst. If a sound hits you in the heart, it hits you in the heart and there's nothing you can do about it. It's the same thing with art, really, but a lot of people aren't exposed to art on a daily basis. That's the thing about music; it doesn't make no sense, rhyme or reason, but when it hits you, you feel no pain.

Rock 'n' Roll got people motivated to want to talk to girls *and* change society. That's when people started feeling that they could take music beyond 'I love her, she doesn't love me' or whatever. You had people saying, 'The police just beat up my cousin.' Why? 'Because he's black.' Or 'My cousin was just hanged.' Why? 'Because he's black.' It's horrifying to think it now, but the last known Ku Klux Klan lynching was in 1981.

Woody Guthrie and Bob Dylan were the leading white male voices in protest music, with Lennon bringing up the rear later on in the Sixties. But even before them, Frank Sinatra more than did his bit. You think of Sinatra and you think of the suit and the hat and the women. But he was a champion of civil rights as far back as 1946, when a documentary he made on race relations won a special Academy Award. He refused to play segregated venues or stay in hotels that refused black people, and once threatened to cause a stink if his friend Lena Horne wasn't allowed into Vegas's whites-only Stork Club. Not only did he perform with the leading black musicians of the day, citing Billie Holiday as his key influence, but he also insisted on integrated orchestras. On one hand, it ensured these musicians got a great gig, on the other it sent a clear message to his fans. Racism wasn't welcome in Frank Sinatra's vision of America. 'A friend to me has no race, no class and belongs to no minority,' he told *Ebony* magazine in 1959. 'My friendships are formed out of affection, mutual respect and something in common. These are eternal values that cannot be classified.' In 1961 he played a benefit show for Martin Luther King Jr, and was such a generous benefactor to the cause that his support was recognized by a lifetime award from the Los Angeles NAACP.

The Chairman stuck his neck out long before it was trendy or cool or even safe to do so. Perhaps Frank knew he could get away a little more than most because he was a big star, and he definitely got away with a hell of a lot because he was a blue-eyed white guy; but you can't diminish his contribution. That said, consider Billie Holiday's 'Strange Fruit' – a black female Jazz artist is taking a much bigger risk than a white young male popular music singer. Billie felt an obligation as a human being and a black American to speak out. So did, in later years, Sam Cooke and Ray Charles. These folk went out of their way to write and record songs that meant a lot to the Civil Rights Movement and their own circumstances, knowing that they would put themselves in the firing line because of it.

There's still a lot of racism, both in music and beyond. We saw the unrest in Ferguson in Missouri in 2014, which is still ongoing, and we know the feeling towards Muslims every time an attack by religious extremists takes place. But if it's fucked up now, imagine what it was like back then. People were existing in an almost apartheid state – you weren't allowed to drink at the same water fountains – and it became the musician's job to play for these people who were being oppressed. When you look at what's going on in the world, it's painful right now. Music is supposed to reflect what society is going through – that's how it's always been. But at the moment it feels like we're passive-aggressively fighting the power; there's no gas in the tank any more, we're coasting but something's got to happen. It always does.

That's the great thing about music. With every generation, something happens: it feels like it's a long time coming but I have hope for this next generation. Someone's going to say something soon that's going to make our jaws drop. Where are the Tracy Chapmans and Tupacs, Lauryn Hills and Chuck Ds of this generation?

You have people selling millions of albums who are really in a position to say whatever they want, and people will listen to them. They've just decided that they are not inclined to do so. Lady Gaga in her own way, with her meat-dress statements and her advocacy of gay rights, is doing something, but she's outnumbered by the rest of them. I don't see a lot of people coming out against the anti-Muslim sentiment in the world today. I don't see people putting out powerful music on major labels any more. I guess, in some respect, you can't blame artists. When the Dixie Chicks spoke out against George W Bush, they got slammed and that was their career off the rails in the States. So now it's so much easier to put on the blinders. Gary Barlow isn't going to write a song about a war vet coming home and trying to find his way again. Top 40 artists aren't talking about domestic violence – I mean even Rihanna, who got the shit kicked out of her by her boyfriend, didn't address it within her music in even a remotely meaningful way. And yet she gives off such a kick-ass Rock 'n' Roll attitude. I hope she doesn't get too lost before she decides to really say something.

We're ready for a shift in music; we're ready for new voices to say real things. We need it, and soon.

*

TALKIN' 'BOUT A REVOLUTION

The emotion that singers like Nina Simone, Ella Fitzgerald, Billie Holiday and Odetta captured was not only undeniable, it was inspiring. Through these women and their songs, many, many people were moved – intellectually and emotionally. You heard the songs they sang and your heart told you that society was wrong and it was up to us to change it. Together we stand, divided we fall.

Odetta was born on New Year's Eve in Birmingham, Alabama, in 1930, and grew up during the Great Depression. It was the protest songs that she heard during those times that would later inspire her in life.

'They were liberation songs,' she told the *New York Times* in 2007. 'You're walking down life's road, society's foot is on your throat, every which way you turn you can't get from under that foot. And you reach a fork in the road and you can either lie down and die or insist upon your life... those people who made up the songs were the ones who insisted upon life.'

Following the death of her father, Odetta and her family relocated to California. Though the racism there wasn't as pronounced as in the South, she experienced segregation first-hand when she wasn't allowed to attend Marshall High School because, she told the *LA Times*, 'they didn't let coloured people go there'. She made it to university, however, and afterwards went on the road with *Finian's Rainbow*, a musical in which she was a member of the chorus. During a break in the run, she went for a coffee while staying with a friend in San Francisco's

North Beach, and it was in this particularly bohemian café that she encountered Folk music for the first time.

'That night I heard hours and hours of songs that really touched where I live,' she told the *LA Times*. 'I borrowed a guitar and learned three chords, and started to sing at parties... As I did those songs, I could work on my hate and fury without being antisocial. Through those songs, I learned things about the history of black people in this country that the historians in school had not been willing to tell us about or had lied about.'

In 1956, Odetta released *Odetta Sings Ballads and Blues*. It was a huge hit in Folk music; Bob Dylan later cited it as not just a huge influence, but actually the record that turned him on to Folk music. After hearing that album, he traded his electric guitar for an acoustic one. So it was through Odetta that we were given 'Blowin' in the Wind', and through Dylan that we got 'A Change is Gonna Come' from Sam Cooke. Tracy Chapman and Janis Joplin were two other artists to be greatly influenced by Odetta's stirring vocals and conscious message. During the Sixties, Odetta became known as the soundtrack to the Civil Rights Movement, with numerous key performances – a particularly memorable one was in 1963 on the steps of the Lincoln Memorial after an introduction by Martin Luther King Jr.

Odetta is one of the few artists in this book who, thankfully, didn't meet a premature end: she died aged 77 of heart disease, but passed away knowing that what she had done had, in its own way, changed the world. I think the late, great Maya Angelou said it best when she said, 'Thank you, Odetta, for continuing to define and enlighten our load.'

*

INNER CITY BLUES

For me, when it comes to the men who produced socially conscious music, it was Stevie Wonder, Curtis Mayfield, Marvin Gaye and Sam Cooke who really brought the goods – all of whom for the most part produced and wrote and recorded everything themselves. They influenced people so greatly and so positively but also so singularly.

Marvin Gaye made a huge impact on me with 1971's *What's Going On*, one of the best albums Motown ever put out. It's beautiful music. Talk about touching all the bases: it touched the human-rights angle, the civil-rights angle and even ecology. He was talking to humans but he was also addressing the environment. When he first started out, Gaye was just getting in there, being a singer, being a songwriter, playing the Motown game. Then, when he became known for hits like 'I Heard It Through the Grapevine' and 'Ain't No Mountain High Enough', Gaye became eager to record music with more depth; something that carried weight.

We might have never even had *What's Going On*, though. Motown, at that time, wasn't interested in promoting a political activist who was making millions for them on the Pop charts. Thank God Marvin stuck to his guns, because that album's power and relevance is still felt today.

The year 1970 was the one that really sparked that change; it had been a tumultuous time for Gaye. His former singing partner and close friend Tammi Terrell had just died of brain cancer, and his brother had recently returned from the Vietnam War. Marvin was also dealing with an insidious cocaine habit – possibly his way of coming to terms with a rough upbringing at the hands of his overbearing, abusive preacher father. He was also going though the gradual breakdown of his marriage with Anna Gordy, sister of Berry Gordy Jr, the owner of Motown, to whom Gaye was signed. In the midst of this personal chaos, there were the enduring echoes of the Watts riots and the assassinations of JFK, MLK and Malcolm X. It was a troubled time both personally and collectively, and Marvin wanted to talk about what was going on. 'My success didn't seem real,' he once said in an interview with biographer David Ritz. 'I didn't deserve it. I knew I could have done more. I felt like a puppet – Berry's puppet, Anna's puppet. I had a mind of my own and I wasn't using it.'

But then along came the track 'What's Going On'. Obie Benson from the Four Tops had the idea for the song after witnessing the police beat on protesters in San Francisco's Haight-Ashbury. Benson worked on the song with Motown's Al Cleveland before taking it to the Four Tops and Joan Baez – both of whom passed. When Gaye heard it, he liked it but wanted to give it to The Originals, a quartet signed to Motown he'd been working with. Benson refused; either Gaye sung it and got credit, or The Originals did and he got none. Marvin agreed to sing it himself and began to add his own touches. 'He added lyrics, and he added some spice to the melody ... He added some things that were more ghetto, more natural, which made it seem more like a story than a song,' Benson told *MOJO* in 1999. 'He made it visual ... When you heard the song you could see the people and feel the hurt and pain.

We measured him for the suit, and he tailored the hell out of it.'

It's crazy to think that when Berry Gordy first heard 'What's Going On', he wasn't sure it should be released. Gaye had called him in Bermuda where Gordy was on holiday and Gordy's initial reaction was that people wouldn't understand. Marvin wasn't known as a political singer, and Motown weren't trying to be a progressive label. Allegedly, Gaye refused to record any more music, so the label reluctantly released the song (Gordy firmly denies this version of events) – and it was an instant smash. The track sold 200,000 copies in one day, giving Gaye the green light to release one of music's most impactful albums.

In the *What's Going On* album, Gaye covered a realm of righteous causes, addressing the environment on 'Mercy Mercy Me'; studying social injustice on 'Inner City Blues'; discussing his own addiction on 'Flyin' High'. He talked about pollution, urban decay, war, religion and love, but without bitterness, always with a sense of possibility.

He took on everything that was going on around him in the world, and had an opinion on it. There was no looking to other people to see the consensus and siding with that: he saw what was going on around him and spoke his mind. 'I don't make records for pleasure. I did when I was a younger artist, but I don't today – I make records that can feed people what they need, what they feel,' Gaye told the *NME* in 1982. 'Hopefully I can record so I can help someone overcome a bad time.' He wrote many more classics, though generally of a more romantic nature – the Grammy-Award-winning 'Sexual Healing' probably being the most well-known.

His 1983 album, *Midnight Love*, released after a period as a tax exile in Europe, was another hit. But while touring with this album Gaye began to unravel and cocaine-fuelled paranoia took hold. He started dropping his pants on stage, collecting guns, wearing a bulletproof vest and acting all erratic and crazy. In an attempt to finally get clean, he went home to his parents' house.

Gaye's relationship with his father had long been fraught and it had worsened when his father had refused to look after his mother following an operation. Living at home with resentment building towards his father, as well as a fierce cocaine habit, things began to spiral. There was talk of suicide attempts – one friend said Gaye had tried to throw himself out of a moving car.

I guess, in the end, it all got too much. The day before his 45th birthday in April 1984, Gaye had an argument with his father, which turned into a physical fight between the two. His father shot him in the chest. According to Gaye's brother Frankie, who held Marvin in his final moments, his last words were: 'I got what I wanted... I couldn't do it myself, so I made him do it.'

Whether or not Gaye Senior killed his son in cold blood, or whether Marvin begged him to pull the trigger, I guess we'll never know.

Although often the first thing that comes to mind when you hear the name Marvin Gaye is that he was murdered by his own father, rather than focusing on that, we should celebrate and spread the word about the legacy that he left. Artists like Marvin Gaye and albums like *What's Going On* are a rarity these days, and we should preserve that memory for ever.

*

FIGHT THE POWER

It's hard to imagine now, but Sam Cooke took a real risk when he recorded 'A Change is Gonna Come'. For a black artist to cross over to a mainstream white audience in the Fifties, as Sam had, was almost impossible.

I reckon Cooke had always been a special dude. There's a story that his brother, LC, tells about Sam in Peter Guralnick's biography, *Dream Boogie*. LC was seven and Sam nine, and Sam was telling his little brother how he had it all worked out. 'I figured out the whole system. It's designed, if you work, to keep you working. All you do is live from payday to payday.' His brother asked him what he was going to do and Sam said, 'I'm gonna sing, and I'm going to make me a lot of money.'

The nine-year-old ambitious kid who had the system figured went on to be very wealthy.

Sam was from a very religious family and had been, until the mid-Fifties, a highly regarded Gospel singer. He released his first Pop single under the name Dale Cook, so as not to alienate his Gospel fans, but there's no disguising that tenor: you can tell Cooke's vocal a mile off. His first record under his own name, 1957's 'You Send Me' on Keen Records, spent weeks at number one on the *Billboard* chart and sold an estimated 1.7 million copies, making it one of the biggest-selling singles of the day. Later came hits like 'Twistin' the Night Away', 'Cupid' and 'Bring It on Home to Me'. With 30 hits in the US Pop charts during his lifetime, Cooke was a pretty big deal. He was making a lot of money for a lot of people, not least himself. So to risk everything to make a political statement was not something he undertook lightly.

There were two things that led Cooke to create the song that would become an anthem for the Civil Rights Movement. The first was Bob Dylan's 'Blowin' in the Wind'. A poignant, poetic strike for civil rights, but Cooke was disappointed that the song hadn't come from a black artist first. Then, in 1963, while on tour, he and his band, and his wife Barbara, were turned away from a Holiday Inn in Shreveport, Louisiana. Cooke was so upset that he refused to leave, and things began to escalate. His wife warned him that he could be killed if he continued to argue. 'They're not gonna kill me, I'm Sam Cooke,' he exclaimed. 'No, to them you're just another... you know.' Cooke was arrested and spent the night in jail for disturbing the peace.

The suffering and humiliation that black people were going through on a daily basis back then gave gasoline to these engines of artistic endeavours. It's hateful that Cooke had to go through that, but thank God it meant he was able to produce such a powerful protest song. It's still so resonant five decades later.

'A Change is Gonna Come' has the most beautiful arrangement; it's a symphony in three and a bit minutes. It has such an epic feel, sonically, but the instrumentation manages never to detract from the message. Cooke performed the song on *The Tonight Show* in 1964 (sadly the network didn't keep the tape), but never performed it live afterwards. He played it to his then-protégé Bobby Womack (who would go on to marry Barbara after Sam's murder). Womack said, 'It sounds like death', to which Sam replied, 'Man, that's kind of how it sounds like to me. That's why I'm never going to play it in public.'

He played it once and never got to perform it again.

In a horrible twist of fate, Sam was shot to death right before the release of the single in 1964. His murder remains one of music's most mysterious deaths, one that is shrouded in strange details and a hasty inquest.

Cooke may have been a religious man, but he was known for loving the ladies too. The guy was, by all accounts, a bit of a player. He was married twice and had numerous girlfriends. On the night of his death, he was sinking martinis in Martoni's, a popular Italian in LA. A pretty 22-year-old, Elisa Boyer, caught his eye, and before long the pair were cozied up in a booth. Around 1am, they moved on to the notorious Rat Pack hangout, PJ's, where Cooke got into an argument with a man who he thought was trying to hit on Boyer. The couple left around 2am and got into Cooke's car, driving to a fleapit motel near LAX called the Hacienda. Leaving Boyer in the car, Cooke went and checked in. The manager, Bertha Franklin, told him only married couples were allowed. He checked in under the name of Mr and Mrs Sam Cooke.

Boyer later claimed that it was when they got to the room that she became afraid that Cooke, who was becoming incredibly aggressive, was going to rape her. As soon as he went into the bathroom, she gathered up her clothes and ran to the manager's office. There was no answer, so she continued to a payphone, where she called the police. In the interim, Cooke had discovered her missing and gone to the office. He was wearing one shoe and a sports jacket; Boyer later said she had accidentally gathered up his shirt and trousers when she'd made her escape.

Cooke began to fight with Bertha Franklin, demanding she tell him where Boyer was. Fearing for her life, Franklin got hold of her pistol and shot Cooke three times. The last bullet entered his left side, passing through his left lung, his heart and his right lung. His final words, according to Franklin, were, 'Lady, you shot me.' He got up once more and ran at her; she hit him over the head with a broom handle. When the police arrived, Sam Cooke was dead. His death was ruled as justifiable homicide, despite there being many inconsistencies and oddities. Some theories suggest that Cooke was set up, that his death was a planned assassination. Others shrug it off as merely a robbery gone wrong.

It's sad that Sam didn't get to see how important his song became – not only to the Civil Rights Movement of the Sixties, but for generations to come. 'A Change is Gonna Come' exemplified the era it was written in, yet transcended that moment in history to have continued relevance, thanks to the dignity and optimism that Cooke managed so effortlessly to convey.

*

GENIUS LOVES COMPANY

If you play 'Georgia on My Mind' and you're not moved by Ray Charles's vocal performance, then you're not in touch with yourself. Or life!

Ray Charles may have been known for being a little crazy – watch the film *Ray* if you haven't already – but guys like him got away with it because they brought it. Really brought it. They came through when they needed to come through.

Ray was banned from playing at the Bell Auditorium in Georgia in 1961 because, it was alleged, he 'broke his contract'. In fact, he had refused to play the Bell because it was segregated. He was fined $800 and told he would never play the Bell again. 'Georgia on My Mind', a song written by Hoagy Carmichael and Stuart Gorrell but predominantly associated with Ray Charles, is now the Georgia state anthem – in a nice ironic twist.

There's a scene in *Ray* where Atlantic's Ahmet Ertegün is playing him a song called 'Mess Around'. Ertegün starts singing it, and then Ray takes over, and you can see Ertegün's like, 'That's the way it's supposed to be done.' If you have all the right ingredients but you're not a chef, chances are you might fuck up. But if you are a chef and you have the right ingredients, then you're going to have yourself a feast.

In a similar way to Sam Cooke and James Brown, Ray Charles was a guy who infused Gospel with Rock 'n' Roll, capturing a rebel spirit with a spiritual sensibility. And like Cooke, Ray risked alienating his R&B audience in 1962 when he decided to release a Country album, *Modern Sounds in Country and Western Music*. For a black artist to try to make Country music was unheard of. He need not have worried: 'I Can't Stop Loving You' sold over a million copies on its release. Ray had an innate ability and talent that allowed him to roam from Pop to Folk to Country to Jazz to Blues and Big Band. Here was a musician who wandered wherever he wanted to and mastered it each time – partly because he was a sublime producer and arranger, but partly because of his voice. 'I can still sing my ass off,' he said in later days. In the industry he was referred to as 'The Genius'. He didn't appear to disagree, titling one of his albums *The Genius of Ray Charles*. 'I was born with music inside of me,' Ray told his biographer, David Ritz, who wrote the as-told-to autobiography *Brother Ray*. 'Music was one of my parts. Like my ribs, my liver, my kidneys, my heart. Like my blood.'

Ray lost his sight early on; one of the last things he saw was the death of his younger brother. Ray, five, was playing in the washtub with George, four. By the time Ray realized that his brother was drowning and had called for his mother, it was too late. 'I can see it all too vividly,' he told Ritz. 'It shines inside my head... It was a powerful thing to have witnessed... Turned out to be one of the last things I would ever see.'

He began to lose his sight shortly afterwards; within two years, Ray was fully blind. He didn't let the loss of his sight hold him back, though. At St Augustine School for the deaf and the blind, he learned Braille and was taught classical piano; when he was supposed to be practising, Ray would dig into Jazz, Boogie-Woogie and the Blues. He taught himself to walk unaided by sticks or dogs, growing increasingly into a talented, confident young man.

After the death of his mother when he was 15, Ray moved to Florida and began getting gigs. It was around this time that he picked up a heroin addiction; being blind, he'd have to get other people to inject for him. His career was nearly ruined in 1964 when he was arrested for possession of heroin and marijuana, but he kicked the habit eventually.

Though he started out imitating Nat King Cole, Ray soon found his own voice and got his first R&B hit with the aforementioned 'Mess Around', and from there we got hit after hit: 'I Got a Woman', 'What'd I Say', 'Hit the Road Jack' and his version of 'Georgia on My Mind'.

`Ray had grown up so poor that he was known to say, 'Even the blacks looked down on us.' He suffered two huge traumatic events in his childhood and had lost both parents by the time he was 15. Being denied sight as a child – that alone could drive a person to madness. But Ray Charles aspired to greatness instead and he achieved it. He refused to accept that the limitations of blindness or society's ignorance about disability should hold him back. Sure, he walked up to that line a few times, but he never crossed it. I guess he'd already seen the abyss when his brother died and he knew what was down there.

In the end, Ray died of liver failure in 2004. He had recorded over 60 albums and performed more than 10,000 shows. But beyond the records sold and the shows played, Ray Charles was a true – and rare – genius of music, and an advocate of breaking the rules with abandon.

*

MUSIC TO DIE FOR

John Lennon had a real idea of what the world should be like and he did everything he possibly could to achieve that vision. He was seeking a world without war, racial division or injustice, poverty or hunger.

There weren't many white musicians who would put their dicks on the chopping block like Lennon did. Here's a guy who gave his MBE back to the Queen in protest at Great Britain supporting the Vietnam War. He and Yoko staged two 'Bed-Ins for Peace' in 1969 – one at the Amsterdam Hilton and one in Montreal – inviting the world's press, and Lennon said, 'There's many ways of protest, and this is one of them... We think that peace is only got by peaceful methods, and to fight the establishment with their own weapons is no good, because they always win, and they have been winning for thousands of years.' At their second bed-in, he performed 'Give Peace a Chance' with Yoko, a song that would become the ultimate anti-war anthem. At the 2012 London Olympics, which showcased Britain's cultural and political advancements, the words Lennon had written back in the Seventies still held real weight when, at the conclusion of the games, they played 'Give Peace a Chance'.

Lennon walked shoulder to shoulder with the Black Panthers and radicals like Abbie Hoffman and Jerry Rubin. He was outspoken: he didn't just write and record a few songs; he was both an on-the-ground activist and a generous donor, financially, to the cause. We all know 'Imagine' and 'Give Peace a Chance', but he also wrote 'Gimme Some Truth', 'Working Class Hero' and even 'Mother', about primal therapy.

A lot of people back in the Seventies thought that guys who spoke out, like Lennon, were out of their minds. But he didn't give a damn. 'Imagine' was a benchmark in white consciousness. I say that because black consciousness always existed – when you've been oppressed for centuries, you're constantly aware of the injustices of the world. 'Imagine', aside from having some of the best lyrics ever written, was also available to everybody's understanding. Just the word 'imagine' took an idea that came from Martin Luther King Jr's 'I Have a Dream' speech. You can see the natural progression of what was going on there. And at that time people were getting killed for their beliefs, for rocking the boat, for throwing rocks at glass houses. Martin Luther King Jr,

Malcolm X, Bobby Kennedy, John F. Kennedy... All these guys who were trying to stand up for what was right were getting murdered. But coming through were Lennon, Cooke, Odetta and Marvin Gaye, all prepared to stand up and be counted despite the risk to their own lives.

I don't see people now who challenge authority in that respect. Especially when it comes to politics and how we do things. There's less and less of that nowadays. People roll their eyes when you say the name 'Bono'. And they shouldn't. At least we've got one. One guy going out and saying, 'This is fucked up – let's change this and make it better.' Bill Gates gave a billion dollars away. Sure, he has a whole lot of billions but we don't look at him as a great guy; we look at him as some nerd with glasses who started Microsoft, which got its ass kicked by Apple.

You can write Lennon off as a hippy whose music was reductive. But that's woefully misunderstating his contribution not only to music but also to culture and politics. His challenges to The Man didn't go unnoticed. It emerged in later years that a memo was sent to the US Attorney General in 1972 citing Lennon as a threat to the re-election of Richard Nixon. The US Immigration Service began a campaign to deport Lennon based on drug possession. Though the case was eventually overturned and Lennon went on to attend the Watergate hearings in 1973, and flash the 'Peace' sign at the Statue of Liberty in 1974, it emerged the FBI had had a huge dossier on him. So much for the harmless hippy who sang about peace.

Although freedom of speech is in the US Constitutional Amendments, it feels at times that it is perhaps more a concept than a right. One that too many people have paid for with their lives.

*

ALL EYEZ ON ME

Hip-Hop was a big part of my life growing up in the Lower East Side of New York, on the fringes of Alphabet City. I grew up around black kids and white kids, Jews, Puerto Ricans and Chinese kids. I'd hear Hip-Hop coming out of car speakers all day long and watch young black and Puerto Ricans B-boy on the block. When we set up Fun Lovin' Criminals, Hip-Hop was a major influence on our songs.

Hip-Hop took its cues from elsewhere, from the likes of James Brown and The Last Poets, Gil Scott-Heron and Baby Huey, who were all precursors of the MC; these guys were rapping years before Big Bank Hank or Doug E Fresh.

Hip-Hop is a direct descendent of spirituals and the Blues. Like the Blues before it, Hip-Hop was, in its early years, very much a communication tool between neighbourhoods. The Bronx could communicate to Brooklyn over vinyl and tapes; it was very parochial. It went from a communication tool to a modern-day form of the Blues – 'This is what's happening here; here's how we feel.' That was really important in Hip-Hop. It would more often than not look at politics and talk about the mayor or about the cop on the corner, or about which gang was the biggest and baddest. 'The Message' by Grandmaster Flash and the Furious Five, released in 1982, is the first well-known socio-political single in Hip-Hop, but they weren't alone back then. Though a lot of early Hip-Hop was about getting the party started and bragging about why you and your neighbourhood were the illest, artists like

Whodini, and later MC Lyte and Big Daddy Kane, also dropped some knowledge for the brain. Afrika Bambaataa broke away from one of America's most feared street gangs, The Black Spades, and formed the Zulu Nation, a legitimate socially conscious movement designed to inspire and motivate young kids.

If you were a young black person in Seventies inner-city America, you had very limited options. If you were offered the chance to become a performer with the possibility of making money, you were going to take that option and work it really hard. Not because you were a money-mad jerk, but because it was an opportunity. Hip-Hop was an opportunity for a lot of people who were amazing musicians to become stars, to be legendary figures in our society. In the Nineties you had Biggie, The Notorious B.I.G., slinging on the corner, but he also had this talent. He had his friends telling him, 'Dude, stop selling dope, go rap about it.' For a young, working-class black kid from the block, Hip-Hop and sport became two viable, if limited, options. Like Biggie said on 'Things Done Changed', 'If I wasn't in the rap game, I'd probably have a key knee-deep in the crack game, 'Cos the streets is a short stop, Either you're slinging crack rock or you got a wicked jump shot.' Hip-Hop became a saviour and salvation for those kids with the talent, wherewithal and opportunity to speak to the people, for the people, about the people.

A lot of people don't link Hip-Hop to the Blues, but it was the same language, the same attitude, the same plain and simple stories, but in a different sonic medium. The early guys of Hip-Hop were storytellers. If you could spit, then you got out of being a stick-up kid. You're an intelligent kid that can't afford college? Music could pay your tuition.

They were ahead of their time and that showed in the endorsements that they got from the likes of the Stones. They fused Rock and R & B effortlessly and created a whole new world.

Jimi took the guitar to the next level. Hendrix and his Strat are as iconic as Michael Jackson's Moonwalk or James Brown and his jumpsuits.

Hearing Janis Joplin sing is pure, unadulterated emotion. It's a sensory overload.

Nico was pre-goth goth! She was contrary, and I like that about her.

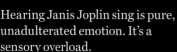

John Lennon had a profound idea of what the world should be like and he did everything he possibly could to do achieve that.

Mama Cass – AKA Cass Elliot – seemed to spend her entire career battling against the perception of an acceptable pop star image. The absolute antithesis of what was being sold as sexy, she was just awesome.

There was Jimi Hendrix and then there was Duane Allman. People see them as waypoints in guitar playing. He was one of those losses that people – that music – really felt.

Drugs took some of our greats before they even had the chance to be great. Baby Huey might remain largely unknown, but that 400 pounds of Soul is felt in music to this day.

Barry White was so real. He was singing the Blues that we could dance to.

The Stones didn't just walk into the Rock 'N' Roll hall of fame, they really had to prove themselves as a world-class, legendary band. They were more rooted in the Blues than the Beatles, and I think that's helped them to live as a band as long as they have.

We really needed Sid Vicious. He couldn't play, but music needed him; his charisma and attitude were it.

They say you should never meet your idols. In Joe Strummer's case it was one of the best things that ever happened to me as a musician.

Prince is the guy who learned from everybody's mistakes, studied them and didn't make them. He's the last Rock star walking around that can enter a room and fuck it up.

Amy Winehouse was a tortured soul. My memory of her was that she might have been messed up, but she was still on point.

He was a smart motherfucker, but people paid more attention to him when he was yelling than when he was articulate. It was a conscious choice for him to go 'thug life'.

Kurt's death symbolized the death of the rebellious spirit and with it, the sense of individual identity and inherent creativity.

As Hip-Hop matured through the Eighties, it got progressively more provocative – sonically and politically. Look at N.W.A.: that was as confrontational as you could get. Public Enemy took it to a very articulate level with their crazy wall of sound produced by The Bomb Squad. The ones that we remember are the ones that back it up with good music. When Hip-Hop was political, it was at its best, in my opinion. Was Hip-Hop something that got co-opted in the same way that Rock 'n' Roll got co-opted? Yeah. Money can infect great music and turn its branches rotten from within. Public Enemy wouldn't get signed now. There's no place for a Public Enemy on a major record label now and there's no place for a Chuck D.

*

THUG LIFE

When he was ten, a minister asked Tupac what he wanted to be when he grew up. 'A revolutionary' was his reply.

Tupac Amaru Shakur was a smart dude. The only reason he thugged it was because he recognized that people paid more attention to him when he was yelling than when he was speaking articulately. It was a conscious choice for him to go Thug Life. As I say, smart dude. His mother, Afeni Shakur, was a Black Panther and she instilled in him that it was crucial to put your point across effectively.

Oftentimes he was reduced to being a gangsta, a thug, a banger. In fact, Pac had a progressive upbringing. Any bad behaviour was rewarded with having to read the *New York Times* cover to cover. He was intelligent, well read and would reference the likes of Shakespeare in interviews once he became famous. He was brought up around the Panthers' ethos, but he was also into the arts and won a place at the Baltimore School for the Arts. But if his initial ambition had anything to do with fame and fortune, his later aspirations were much more to do with empowerment and enlightenment. He may not have presented his ideas with hearts and flowers, but his narrative was persuasive, it was thrilling, it was needed. He talked about single mothers and teenage pregnancy, police abuse and racial profiling. In the midst of this were lyrics that were misogynistic and menacing and, well, pretty fucking violent. But the dichotomy of his character was what made Pac so alluring. He grew up around politicized intellectualism but also pronounced thug life and gangsterism. He called women bitches but then wrote 'Brenda's Got a Baby'. He was an artist and expressed himself as such. I might not always have loved everything Pac said, but I respected his right to express himself and hoped that not everything he said was to be taken literally. Some of his vernacular seemed to be simply what was expected of him as a rapper; in order to draw people in and hit them with the good stuff, you needed the hook for the bait.

And he gave a shit. The media covered his numerous fights and visits to jail, but ignored the fact he'd fly across the country to meet a dying kid. Or that he would spend Thanksgiving helping to pass out thousands of dollars' worth of turkeys to people in South Central. He took the stepdaughter of a murdered friend to a prom. One night, while at LA's House of Blues, he noticed nobody was dancing with a woman in a wheelchair. He spent the next four hours dancing with that woman.

He financed an at-risk youth centre and bankrolled a South Central sports team.

A lot of things changed in Hip-Hop back in '96 and '97 when Tupac and Biggie were shot and killed. A lot of popular Hip-Hop descended into mediocrity and mindlessness. Sure, Big and Pac rapped about hoes and money. They had an intellect and a sense of style, flair, innovation... So when Pac did speak out about the black experience, people really listened.

Tupac knew he didn't have long on this earth – he often prophesied his own death in both interviews and his videos, predicting he would be 'in the cemetery' within 15 years in one interview with *Entertainment Weekly*. He was just 25 years old when he was shot in a drive-by. He died six days later. His death was not only a loss to Hip-Hop, but also a loss to music. Pac was one of Hip-Hop's most powerful orators and narrators. He was incredibly charismatic and articulate. In many ways, he was a griot as much as a rapper, and he was forceful in the delivery of his message. That voice, that energy, that persuasiveness, is sadly missing in rap nowadays. Though there are some rhymers out there, like Pharoahe Monch, Kendrick Lamar and J Cole, they are few and far between. The major labels aren't signing them; it seems that the machine is only interested in producing cookie-cutter rappers who can tell us how many clothing brands they own.

I'd love to know what Tupac would be up to today if he'd made it. Something tells me he'd still be stirring shit up, causing a ruckus. If he were around, a lot of rappers wouldn't be getting up to the shit they get up to, selling the culture out, because Pac would be calling them out on it.

But he has gone and now we need the new Tupac Shakur to take up the mantle. If Hip-Hop can't provide a voice for this generation, I'm not sure who can.

EXCESS ALL AREAS: NEW YORK STATE OF MIND

I could write a whole book just on New York City. It's the place I was born and it's the place where I grew up. So much happened to me in that town: I got girls, got my heart broke, broke a couple of hearts, got drunk, got high, got arrested, got into music, joined the Marines, put a band together... You can live a whole lifetime there before you're out of your teens. It's a cliché, but you can take the man out of Manhattan – you'll never take Manhattan out of the man. Where I live now, in Somerset, couldn't be more different, but New York is who I am, who I'll always be. When you meet someone born and bred in New York, you can spot them a mile off. We just give off that New York air.

I grew up in Manhattan's Lower East Side. It was a pretty deep neighbourhood back then. We didn't know they had changed the colour of NYPD's cars from dark green to blue and white until we saw it on TV. Police cars never came round our way. They were paid to stay away.

Even though I lived in a pretty rough neighbourhood, we weren't particularly poor; my mom was just hip like that, wanting to live downtown. My mom did OK for herself. She was a great mom; she'd take me to museums and we'd travel a lot. I saw lots of different sides of New York City as a kid and I had friends who came from all walks of life. Growing up in Seventies and Eighties New York was a pretty wild ride. Me and my buddies would wander around the city's streets, getting high and just being assholes. Pimps, hookers, hustlers and dealers were the norm. People were being murdered, raped and pillaged all over the city and you could buy drugs on pretty much any corner. There was trash everywhere in the streets and rats roamed freely. It was as close to lawless as you could get in a major metropolis of the Western world.

Growing up in that neighbourhood, we kids didn't see racism. Colour and religion didn't matter in our neighbourhood. Every Friday, one mother in the crew would take all the other kids for a few hours, watch a movie and feed them, while all the other parents could get a couple of hours off. I never knew the difference between black and white and Chinese and Hispanic until I got older and I heard people call each other names. That confused the shit out of me. This was the Eighties, not the Sixties! It goes to show, even in the midst of racial segregation, you'd still get pockets where people would mix it up; Hip-Hop was built on the synthesis of Jamaican, African-American and Puerto Rican kids.

If I think of New York, the year 1973 comes straight to my mind. I was five years old. It's like I have a head camera on and I'm walking around the city, seeing how things were. New York was a very, very different place to what it is now. The heart of the city has completely changed; it's almost unrecognizable. If you want to see New York like I saw it in the Seventies, you'd have to travel into the most remote parts of Queens or Brooklyn or maybe the Bronx. Back then, that seditious city was wild and wonderful and weird; it's no surprise that some of the most important genres of music were born or incubated on the streets of the Rotten Apple.

It was a free-for-all. You could do whatever you wanted to fucking do, whenever you wanted to fucking do it. Whenever I feel homesick, I watch *Taxi Driver* – it reminds me of the New York I grew up in. At one point in the movie, De Niro is walking down 42nd Street and it's all smut films and pimps and nasty places and hookers. That's Times Square! That unbridled flouting of the law continued until Giuliani got into City Hall, in 1994, and started to clean the city up, turning it into the Disneyland that it is today. Today it's all the M&M's store and Calvin Klein ads, teeming with street performers and tourists. Back then the cops let it all go on in the heart of Manhattan, I guess, because it was contained to one area. But I was happy back then *because* New York was so fucked up. For me, the city has lost a lot of its soul.

To see musicians hanging out in New York back then was no big deal. I would often see some of the biggest stars of the Sixties and Seventies, copping drugs, getting drunk or arguing on the street with girlfriends, or just going about their everyday business. The first time I saw Keith Richards was when he walked out of an apartment building on St Mark's and Avenue B. I was in Tompkins Square Park playing basketball and he walked across the street right by us. I was about 10 or 11. We were like, 'Oh, shit – Keith Richards', and carried on playing ball. You'd see all these Rock stars and no one would freak out about it unless they were tourists. Even now, you have a lot of actors and whatever living in New York and no one bugs them. New Yorkers have too much of their own shit to deal with to be bothered by some celebrity buying their groceries.

New York never called itself cool. It was just New York City – the island next to America! Because of the crime, the dirt and the extremes of poverty and wealth, New York and its permissive attitude created a breeding ground for talent and creativity and experimentation, whether it was Harlem and its Jazz clubs in the Thirties and Forties, or later on CBGB's, Studio 54, Tunnel, the Chelsea Hotel and Max's Kansas City, all at the forefront of Punk, Rock, Rap and Disco.

There was always an outside fringe of artists hanging out in NYC. It wasn't the West Coast, all sunshine and palm trees and golden sands. It was cold, it was dingy, it was dark and the cops didn't give a fuck what these kids were doing downtown. They got away with a lot of shit back in the day.

Nowadays New York is really just a homage to wealth and success – but without any contrast. If you live in Manhattan, you have to be very wealthy. You can't live on the Lower East Side any more and not be making $200,000 a year. New York's DIY streak and its irreverent, impulsive, rule-breaking attitude have slowly been eradicated, and that's sad. The New York I know and love was front and centre of some of the most creative counterculture movements of our times.

The city still doesn't sleep, but she's been dozing for a couple of decades. I hope she stops hitting the snooze button soon, because music – as well as art, film and fashion – needs her.

*

LIVING LA VIDA LOCA

Salsa was a big deal where I came from in the LES during the late Sixties and Seventies. There were a lot of Latin-American, Hispanic and African-American people in the neighbourhood, and so this fusion of Salsa and Mambo and later on Disco and Hip-Hop constantly bubbled in the streets. I heard Salsa blaring from apartment blocks in the summer and from car windows in the winter throughout my childhood.

There was so much money in the Salsa scene and to us it was so glitzy. It was very Rock 'n' Roll in that it was incredibly excessive with alcohol and drugs and sex. It had the Rock 'n' Roll attitude and the musicians were really breaking ground. Especially artists like Tito Puente, Héctor Lavoe and Willie Colón – they invented a whole new type of music. It went from Mambo to these guys introducing a new sound, which was termed 'Salsa'.

There was only one label that really mattered in Salsa: Fania Records, owned by an Italian-American lawyer, Jerry Masucci, and a Dominican composer and bandleader, Johnny Pacheco. The pair founded the label in 1964, initially selling records out of the back of a car before signing up the scene's top musicians, including Willie Colón, Celia Cruz, Héctor Lavoe, Eddie Palmieri and Rubén Blades. Anyone who was anyone was on that label; it was the Motown or Def Jam or Blue Note of Salsa.

The Fania All-Stars' *Live in Africa*, recorded live in 1974 in Kinshasa, Zaire, is a great place to start – even though it's without the label's marquee name, Willie Colón, who refused to get on the plane to Africa. Watching his bandmates get their vaccinations before the flight didn't do much for his phobia of needles.

Though he's not on that record, you have to get into Willie Colón. Colón was a Nuyorican (a Puerto Rican born in New York) from the South Bronx, who signed to Fania as a trombonist at the age of 15. He released his first album, *El Malo*, in 1967 at the age of 17. Although critics called it 'amateur', the record sparked a renaissance in Latino music, selling over 300,000 copies on release. *El Malo* was, ostensibly, by teenagers for teenagers, and it opened the door for a whole new generation of Latin-American music fans ready to transition to a more street-oriented Salsa sound.

You should also pick up a copy of *Cosa Nuestra*, recorded with Héctor Lavoe, with whom Willie worked with until Lavoe's drug addiction caused him to miss shows or turn up late. (Lavoe died of AIDS in the early Nineties.) The cover artwork is Colón standing at the foot of the Brooklyn Bridge, trombone case in his hand, cigar in his mouth, looking down at a body wrapped in chains at his feet. This is in 1969. There's another album the pair did a year later in 1970, *La Gran Fuga*, which features Colón's mugshot and a 'Wanted by FBI' sticker saying 'Armed with a trombone and considered dangerous'. These motherfuckers were badass; this was Gangsta Rap before we had Ice-T or N.W.A. Willie, and his partner in crime, Lavoé, were making a heavy-duty statement with their artwork back then: don't fuck with us. Colón was known for fusing his Mambo with R&B, Doo-Wop and Flamenco, but the art direction and attitude of albums like *La Gran*

Fuga channelled Hip-Hop half a decade before the genre even came into existence.

Watch the movie *El Cantante*, starring J Lo and Marc Anthony – purely as a history lesson – because it shows how glitzy and cokey that scene was, and how much money there was in it for those guys. It was very Rock 'n' Roll but it was Latino Rock 'n' Roll. This was another segment of society that was overlooked by the white population, so they could get away, to an extent, with doing what they wanted to do.

Salsa wasn't a music that really went beyond its intended demographic; it was an alternative to Disco for Latinos. It was physical dance music that was very sexual and fuelled by cocaine and rum. The heyday of Salsa was a great period in New York City; at the same time as Talking Heads were doing their thing, you had wild Disco parties uptown at Studio 54, and The Velvet Underground doing God knows what at Max's Kansas City, and you had Latinos bumping and grinding in the seedier parts of town. New York in the Seventies was one long, wild party, mostly uncontrolled by the NYPD and the mayor. Back then, the Mambo and Salsa guys Rock 'n' Rolled it more than the Disco guys did.

Those guys are so important to music but they're mostly overlooked. Tito Puente was the King of Mambo: if you say 'El Rey' anywhere in New York City people know *exactly* who you're talking about. A lot of great musicians are overlooked because of geography. Johnny Hallyday was huge in France from the Sixties onwards, but was unfairly seen as a poor man's Elvis by the rest of the world. The Criminals performed at a festival Hallyday was playing; people were *crying* when he was singing. This guy really touched people. Music can be very parochial.

In the UK – and the US – we look only to ourselves, to music that is innately familiar, for our musicians. What I'm trying to do on my radio show is talk about music that remains largely undiscovered by us. We tend to ghettoize non-American and non-British music and lump it all into 'World Music', which is so reductive. It means lots of us are missing out on some of the most interesting music being made today. There is incredible music in every country, in every home around the world. There are so many artists that just haven't transcended the barriers and borders of their country, or their geographical area, or their racial demographic. And that's where the real legends are. Go to Africa and mention the band Witch and people go crazy. Or Fela Kuti. Go to Cuba and mention Celia Cruz. Or Willie Colón.

I saw recently that Fania has been resurrected, which is super-cool. Though I doubt we'll see an explosion in Salsa and Mambo among the younger generation, it's gratifying that, while this music may be gone, it's certainly not forgotten.

*

I FEEL LOVE

The first record I ever bought was Donna Summer's 'On the Radio'. It was the coolest-looking record ever. I saved up my allowance for three weeks to get a buck fifty together. We had to go to 6th and 7th Avenue, which felt like miles away, to buy the record. This being New York, there was a Latino bookshop opposite the record store, on 14th Street, that Tom Waits used to live above. I used to like to picture him up there, looking down on the city, smoking, drinking, writing songs.

I had tapes, of course – we used to swap tapes all the time – but that was the first record I bought. I'd bought a new record player and I wanted something high-fidelity that would test out the record player. I knew 'On the Radio' would sound good on the system and it did. Now when I have a new stereo, I always test it with Steely Dan's 'Babylon Sisters'.

Donna Summer had a sound; that four-on-the-floor was really tribal. You could hear in Summer's Disco the same stomp that you could hear in the Blues. She always had an inherent melody but also so much feeling and depth. She was singing Disco Blues. 'She Works Hard for the Money' was a proto-feminist record. 'Bad Girls' was about streetwalkers. But Summer was a church girl too: the Gospel-driven 'Forgive Me' earned her a Grammy in 1984.

LaDonna Adrian Gaines was one of seven kids born to a butcher father and a teacher mother in Boston in the late Forties. 'I grew up in a family with five girls and one boy, and we lived in a three-family house, so I had to compete,' she told *Rolling Stone* in 1978. 'To be heard, you had to talk loud. Either that or you just tried to find a hollow corner where you could sit and fantasize about being someplace else. And school wasn't any easier. I went to school with some pretty violent people, and I was an outsider because I couldn't live on that black-and-white separatist premise. Racial? I didn't know what the word meant until I was older.'

In 1957, when she was eight, Summer performed at the Grant AME Church. She stood in for another member of the congregation who was sick, singing Mahalia Jackson's 'I Found the Answer'. 'And during the course of that song,' Summer told the *Daily Telegraph* in 2008, 'I heard a voice in my head say to me, "You're going to be famous. This is power, and be careful never to misuse this power." Now, to me it was the voice of God. There was such an authority in the voice, I just started crying.'

When she opened her eyes, the congregation was also in tears.

As a teen, Summer joined a Blues and Rock band called Crow. Featuring a racially diverse line-up – Donna on vocals of course – the comparatively progressive Crow preceded the likes of Rufus and Chaka Khan. Though they were offered a deal with RCA, the group split and Donna successfully auditioned to play Sheila in the Munich production of *Hair*. At the age of 18, Gaines left the US for Germany.

She became fluent in German, met her husband, Helmuth Sommer, took his name and swapped the 'o' to an 'u', had a child and set up home. It was through being a session singer in Munich that she met producer Giorgio Moroder and songwriter Pete Bellotte and her fate was sealed. In 1975 she became a huge star when 'Love to Love You Baby', with its 20-plus simulated orgasms, became an international hit.

She was a special lady, Donna Summer. What Moroder, Bellotte and Summer did was so tight. The music they made epitomized the hedonism and rampant sense of sexual freedom that was rife in the Seventies. Summer was, however, keen to point out that she was also a good Christian. 'I'm not just sex, sex, sex,' she told *Ebony* magazine in 1977. 'I would never want to be a one-dimensional person like that.' She sure was smart; as she felt Disco starting to wane, Summer fused a little Rock guitar into her singles; 1979's 'Hot Stuff' won a Grammy for

Best Female Rock Vocal Performance.

She wasn't just a vocalist for hire; it was Summer who gave Moroder the idea for 'Love to Love You' – he then came in and Morodered it. That record – you think Studio 54. It takes you right back to where you were when you heard it, yet it's so timeless. That's why music is so important. As a musician, you're taking a snapshot of who you are at that moment. Your intellect, your stupidity – whatever it is. I look back on our Fun Lovin' Criminals records and I like that kid. He was trying! We made cool, singular music; we didn't sound like anybody else. Now it's so samey. When Donna Summer came out, there was no one else like her. So potent were her records that they've been sampled by people as diverse as the Pet Shop Boys and Nas, Beyoncé and Justice.

In the days where Disco vocalists were becoming two-a-penny, it says an awful lot about Summer that she managed to last the distance and stand out so far from the pack. Not only that, but it's also through Summer and Moroder that we saw the foundations of Dance music laid down. They pioneered the 12-inch Dance record with 'Love to Love' and fused American Dance music with European – later inspiring the likes of David Bowie. Her legacy had been set in stone since the Seventies.

When Summer died in 2012, Quincy Jones, who produced albums for her, tweeted: 'Rest in peace dear Donna Summer. Your voice was the heartbeat and soundtrack of a decade.' Aretha Franklin said: 'In the Seventies, she reigned over the disco era and kept the disco jumping. Who will forget "Last Dance"?'

Summer transcended her background, her own expectations and her genre, and to me she'll always be the Queen of Disco. Long may she reign.

*

BIG PIMPIN'

I remember seeing Barry White on the streets of New York when I was – shit – 12 or 13 years old. I was out with my friends, uptown on 57th Street, doing who knows what. I was a little troublemaker back then. I knew who the fuck Barry White was, though. I remember I saw this mountain of a man get out of a car with this serene, beautiful woman. It was like the air around them shifted. As he stood up straight and took the woman's arm, I could see it was Barry White. He was wearing a white suit with a pimp-style winter hat – fur round the brim – and a huge fur coat. His woman was wearing this amazing chinchilla, her high heels clicking alongside White on the sidewalk. I stopped in the street and stared right up at him. 'Are you Barry White, sir?' He looked down. 'Yes, son, I am,' he said in that big, booming, sidewalk-vibratingly low voice. 'I really like your music,' I said. 'Thank you very much, son', and he kept walking. 'He called me son!' I was with my friend Mario – he was like, 'Holy shit, Barry White talked to you!' I was like, 'That's what you get when you're polite to people!'

When you think of Barry White, you get an immediate image, right? You couldn't deny this dude wearing a white leisure suit with a white cape in a great big fucking fur coat with a walking stick and a fedora. You could not deny him that. Some people can't pull that look off. I know I can't. He was a showbiz guy who knew the business because it was a hustle. A lot of these legends made legendary status not just because of their immense talent but because they were hustlers and they knew they could hustle their way in. Barry did everything himself. He even used to press his own records and sell them out of his car for a short time.

Barry White has been a big influence on me. At the time I met him, in my early teens, I was learning to be a musician *because* of musicians like him. So meeting him made a big impression on me even though I was already a fan. The Criminals had a song, 'Love Unlimited', about Barry White and his 40-piece Love Unlimited Orchestra. Barry used to play our song right before he came on stage. The lights would go down and he'd come out to 'Love Unlimited'. He even mentioned it in his memoirs, saying it had 'A great sound, a very funky beat. I love it to death. Thank you, boys.'

Producer, arranger, writer, singer, performer... The man did so many things behind the scenes and in front of the microphone. He wasn't from Philly, but he was bringing that real Philly Soul to Disco and to R&B. It was slowed-down Soul with a Rock edge. His voice was unmistakable and amazing but he also changed the way people wrote songs. He wrote songs for the ladies so the dudes could get down with the girls. I can listen to 'Can't Get Enough of Your Love, Babe' or 'Love's Theme' and think he's written those songs for me. That's what makes great music so great – records that you feel have been written just for you. Barry White made music for real people about real people.

Brought up Barry Eugene Carter in South Central LA, his teenage years were troubled: his brother was killed in a gang fight, and at 17 Barry did some time for stealing car tyres. While he was in prison, he heard Elvis on the radio singing 'It's Now or Never' and I guess he knew he could shake it up. Though he would laugh about the squeaky voice he had as a kid, when he hit his teens his voice broke and that great, rumbling, rough-and-gruff vocal emerged. When he got out of prison, he left gang life behind him, concentrating instead on making his name in music.

I think Barry did so well because he was being real about stuff. He was singing Blues that we could dance to. This was the era of Disco (some pinpoint 'Love's Theme' as Disco's first hit) but his beats weren't compromisingly Disco. There was still a real drummer rocking it, the rhythm section was still real edgy. He made the call on how people would play and he made sure there was a lot of Funk and Blues and Soul in everything he made.

We invented the word 'star' for people like Barry White. He did everything: wrote, arranged, produced, performed, put bands together, made coffee for motherfuckers... and he sang about real shit. 'Never, Never Gonna Give Ya Up' – you know he's stating a fact there. He's made up his mind; the case is closed – he's just giving you a recap. He had this lovely production and he had a vocal that was very low and gruff and really used it in a beautiful, sublime way. He knew what he could do and he did it with love. Number one, he could take you to a place that was safe. Number two, he could tell you a story. Number three, you could listen to it and recognize it as a groove, as a Dance song, but then you could sit back and really listen to it and hear the layers involved in the production. It's deep stuff. Barry White made such a contribution to music as a whole, not only to fans but to future musicians like myself.

*

NEVER MIND THE BOLLOCKS

Punk Rock is a London thing, there's no doubt of that, but there were precursors to the scene that can most definitely be found – and heard – on the streets of New York City.

When the New York Dolls guys first came out, they might have dressed like women – but they'd kick your ass all over St Mark's Place if you said anything about it. They were crazy bastards. They used to have fights with dudes and stomp them out with those big platform shoes. They were respected because they rocked that crazy Glam Rock look with a proto-Punk mentality but also because they played the music that they played, and they backed it up. Every show that the Dolls played, they were on the one. Before these guys came around, there had been a void in music in a lot of ways. People were looking for the new thing and the Dolls were it. And they were amazing.

The Dolls – along with The Velvet Underground and The Stooges – were the dawn of Punk Rock. Malcolm McLaren saw them in New York and when he got back home to England he tried to sign Sylvain Sylvain to front the Sex Pistols – who we'll come to. Sylvain stayed in New York, however, so that line-up never happened.

But the New York Dolls, who formed in 1971 (about four years before the Pistols), did their thing regardless. Sylvain, David Johansen, Billy Murcia and Johnny Thunders were truly Punk Rock. Hanging out at dive bars like Max's Kansas City and CBGB's, they were anti-everything: establishment, The Man, convention, rules...

There was so much talent in that band, but their guitar player, Johnny Thunders, was truly remarkable. People say he was just a 'junkie guitar player', but there was a lot more to Thunders than heroin. Johnny was raw on that Gibson TV Junior; he had the Blues deep inside him. 'The only technical things I know are treble, volume and reverb, that's all,' Johnny once said. He was an Italian-American kid from Queens, and he used to hang out at this Blues bar, Dan Lynch, on 2nd Avenue. I used to go there when I was really young and look in the window; every now and then you'd catch a glimpse of someone famous in there, and more times than not it was Thunders. Or he'd be sat outside, nodding out or whatever.

He had that sensibility as a musician that was so in tune with what the band was doing. And unfortunately he just happened to have a really bad heroin habit. There's a great book that photographer Bob Gruen did about the Dolls that's bound in pink spandex. You see how Johnny went from being a relatively healthy Rock 'n' Roll dude to a skinny junkie dude by the end of the book. I mean, a lot of people at that time returned to the needle, because it was easy to get, it filled that hole. As I said, drugs were rife in New York and ingesting as many as you possibly could was the norm in those circles.

Johnny Thunders was a big inspiration to a lot of guys, because he was such a good guitar player, and he made the Dolls as good as they were. David Johansen was a great frontman and singer, but Johnny Thunders was his Keith Richards.

The Dolls didn't last long; their prophetic second album *Too Much Too Soon* signalled the end for the band, which broke up in 1975.

Thunders went on to form the Heartbreakers with Richard Hell from Television and they kicked ass as a band too.

We don't know when exactly we're going to go, but some people race to the finish, for one reason or another. And some people accidentally finish the race before they've even found their stride, like Jimi or Johnny, who was found dead in a New Orleans guesthouse at the age of 38. When he died, he had been trying to get clean – rumours swirled that his death may have been foul play – but there were large amounts of cocaine and methadone found in his system. We'll perhaps never know. But either way, by then, he'd come, he'd seen and he'd rocked. When he checked out, he'd created a pretty awesome Rock 'n' Roll legacy.

*

Although the Dolls and Johnny Thunders sowed the seeds of the Punk Rock spirit, it was of course an obnoxious band from London who we mostly closely associate with Punk Rock. When you think 'Punk Rock', you think the Sex Pistols and you think Sid Vicious.

Sid is one of the anomalies in this book, in that he proved you didn't have to have innate talent to be an icon or a real Rock 'n' Roller. The Sex Pistols showed us that you didn't even have to know how to play a guitar – you can just pick it up and make it happen. Gary Oldman did a better Sid in the biopic *Sid and Nancy* than Sid did – he played bass better than Sid did, that's for sure! Sid was *never* on the one. But that was what made him important. He was barely in the band, musically, yet he was the figurehead of the Pistols. The rest of the band was really good – they're a tight band – but Sid sucked. All these people that we're talking about were all outside the box. They all went and made great marks on music that we still listen to today, and still speak about. Sid didn't do anything – he was just in the room!

A lot of the Pistols mythology is intrinsically linked to self-harm; the types of things people don't often talk about. A lot of people have those problems and people related to Sid on a lot of different levels: his problems were their problems. He was very honest about the fact that he was messed up; he wasn't shy about it. It was a running joke with the musicians in Punk Rock. He was kind of funky, he smelled funny, he couldn't play bass…

In the mid-1970s, a 17-year-old Sid was hanging around 430 King's Road, aka Vivienne Westwood's Sex shop, busking and meeting like-minded musicians. He stuck up a tatty piece of paper looking for band-members, with the charming postscript, 'No flares. No cripples.' He was the cute young poster boy back then, this was pre-drugs and shit. But it seems like there might have been predisposition to trouble; his mom kicked him out of home at 16 and he'd been assigned a counsellor while studying at Kingsway College. This raffish energy and unpredictability served him well initially; when the Pistols kicked Glen Matlock out, Sid was brought in. He immediately became the front man, the poster boy. He had the look, that skinny-jeans physique that kids are still emulating today. They let him do whatever the fuck he wanted, because he had the look.

To this day people relate to Sid as Punk Rock. I sincerely think he didn't care about anything but getting high. We look on it as a Rock 'n' Roll tragedy that he brought on himself. He couldn't play guitar, he couldn't play a lick, he couldn't write songs. He didn't really do anything except be a stage presence. They'd recut his playing on recordings. He wasn't into learning the bass – he was either too drunk or high to play it.

They used him like an experiment, really. Malcolm McLaren was a fucked-up dude. McLaren encouraged that destructive behaviour in Sid, in a way: take drugs, go break up a hotel in America, spit on people... Knowing that the kids would love it and the rednecks would flip out and they'd have a big media splash. It was smart marketing, I guess.

It's really like we *needed* Sid. As useless as he essentially was, we needed him – we needed the guy who fucked up, who died, who went down in flames. He was a train wreck and everyone knew it. That was how people wanted Punk Rock. It wouldn't be the same without him. His charisma and his attitude were it.

He and Johnny Lydon were best friends and it was when they fell out that things started going wrong with the band. John was trying to do something different, take on social issues like Thatcherism. And we needed someone to do that too – Punk Rock was as important to the working class as some of the civil rights music put out by Marvin Gaye and Curtis Mayfield.

Sid pushed the envelope with his performances, but it got out of control – spitting at the audience, hitting them... Sid was very free, and money was freedom in that respect. He was free to do what he wanted, when he wanted – the records could be made without him being there and he was just needed for shows, to get up there and do something stupid. He wasn't in any way beholden to being a musician; he just had to turn up. Punch in and get fucked up.

I listened to his 1978 version of 'My Way' recently. It was a moment in time when people with influence were starting to be heard. People were beginning to listen to the Pistols via Richard Branson, who had just started Virgin. Branson is a billionaire now – he has an island, an airline, space travel... But this guy was a Punk back in the day; he lived on a houseboat in Little Venice. To have someone from the Punk era be so respected now by the establishment is crazy. It makes you wonder what might have happened to Sid if he'd made it through.

Sid's relationship with Nancy is one we've seen repeated throughout the history of music: Kurt and Courtney, Amy and Blake. When you're in a relationship, the other person can have a serious influence on what you do – especially if you're in a serious relationship, and particularly if you're in a drug-using relationship. Sid and Nancy were fucked up. She was always the one going out and copping for him because he was too famous. They think that's how Nancy got stabbed: someone came to the Chelsea and it was a drug deal gone bad, and she didn't get the stuff and so Sid stabbed her – or so the story goes. Everyone had a pocketknife on them back then.

The Chelsea Hotel was a key part in not only Sid and Nancy's story but also in New York Rock music. There was something about that place. It cut across all class lines with musicians. From Leonard Cohen to Sid, everybody has been there. There was always a lot of bad shit going on at the Chelsea Hotel. It's under new ownership now but you used to see people going up and down elevators, staying in getting drugs, getting deliveries of food if they got hungry, or liquor. It really was a kind of hell.

I'm glad Sid was around, however briefly, to give everyone a kick in the balls. It was getting to a point where there wasn't real rebellion in music. Sid injected life back into it. I think a lot of the pressure was on him and he sought refuge and solace in drugs. He was looking for a way to get away from being 'Sid... crazy Punk guy' and just be Sid. He was a bright kid and when he wasn't high he was a really nice dude but then he'd get drunk and Sid Vicious came in the room. No one can balance that amount of drug intake and the pressures of being a functioning addict with trying to be a professional musician... But it's still unbelievable that he was only 21 when he died.

The Pistols made three LPs. They struck while the iron was hot. Malcolm McLaren had his finger on the pulse. Unfortunately, when Sid's pulse stopped, McLaren's focus shifted. The Pistols were no longer relevant, or important enough. Punk was fading and people were getting down to something else... Hip-Hop was starting to come in, and Electro, and discotheques were in vogue. No one wanted to be spat on by some cocky kid who screamed and could barely play guitar.

Sid died by simply taking a lot of heroin one day. A lot of shit was coming down on him. Maybe it was suicide or maybe he just wanted to take shit and forget about stuff. It was suggested that he killed Nancy so he then killed himself, but I don't know. Either way, Sid checked out early, but he did what he needed to do while he was here. He was – and remains – an icon of Punk Rock and no one can ever take his place.

LEAVING
ON A
JET PLANE

There's a real basic rule if you're a Rock star: don't get on the plane, dude. If it's one of those tiny twin-engine-type tin cans and the weather ain't looking too good and you're famous – take a cab. Cycle. Walk. Miss the show. Do whatever you got to do, but don't get on that plane. Why would a record company or a manager ever hire a jet after Buddy Holly? Just put the motherfucker on a bus. When there are lightning storms, you don't pick up a steel rod and walk down the street, right? You don't tie rocks round your legs if you see a tsunami coming. It's like, 'OK, you're a really great musician – here's a really small plane, and the weather is bad. Off you go.'

We've lost some of our greatest musicians before their time in all manner of ways – drugs, suicide, at the hands of a madman. But damn, we've lost a lot of these guys in freak accidents because of poor judgement: Buddy Holly, Patsy Cline, Otis Redding, Aaliyah, Randy Rhoads, John Denver, Stevie Ray Vaughan, half of Lynyrd Skynyrd… The list goes on.

I'm not scared of flying. I know that it's one of the safest modes of transport; I know you're more likely to die in a car accident than you are a plane crash. But that's for regular folk. If you're a musician, and in particular a young, rich, successful one – don't get on that Beechcraft Bonanza or that Cessna, homie. It's not going to end well.

We'll never know what might have become of these greats, many of whom were taken in their prime. Perhaps they'd still be playing today, maybe they'd have declined into obscurity – it's impossible to say. All I know is, if I see a famous person boarding a small aircraft, I'm absolutely not getting on that motherfucker. And neither should you.

*

THE DAY THE MUSIC DIED

When a Beechcraft Bonanza crashed just outside Clear Lake, Iowa in 1959, we lost three Rock 'n' Roll greats: Buddy Holly, Ritchie Valens and J P Richardson, aka The Big Bopper. Given that this was the beginning of Rock 'n' Roll as we know it, that's some serious talent taken out in the infancy of the game.

Holly, Valens and Richardson were on a tour called the Winter Dance Party: 24 shows all over the Midwest in 24 days. They had been performing at the Surf Ballroom, in Clear Lake, Iowa and were going on to the next show in Moorhead, Minnesota. The tour was taking its toll; it was the dead of a bitter Midwest winter and the guys plus their backing bands had been on the road for nearly two weeks. The crappy tour buses they were travelling on had no heating and they all had colds or flu – one band member was even hospitalized for frostbite. It was freezing cold, it was dark, it was miserable and they hadn't washed their clothes since the start of the tour. Holly wanted to get to Moorhead as soon as possible, get warm and clean and do some washing. So he decided to charter a four-seater plane from nearby Mason City to Fargo, North Dakota. On board with him were Valens (thought to have won his seat in a coin toss) and a flu-ridden Bopper, who was given the seat by a sympathetic Waylon Jennings. Last on board was 21-year-old pilot Roger Peterson, who, it turned out, wasn't certified to fly by instruments only. The plane took off at 12.55am in light snow with strong winds. It crashed shortly after take-off, five miles northwest of the airport. Inclement weather and pilot error were ruled as the cause of the crash.

Because of the late hour, it wasn't until the next day that the wreckage and bodies of the four men were discovered. When Holly's pregnant wife, María Elena, was told of her husband's death, she suffered a miscarriage. Waylon Jennings, who had given up his seat on the plane for The Big Bopper, remembered the final conversation he'd had with Holly. 'I hope your ass freezes on the bus,' Holly had laughed before heading off to take his flight. 'Yeah, well, I hope your plane crashes,' Waylon had retorted. Needless to say, those words haunted him for the rest of his life. 'For years after, I thought I caused [the crash],' Jennings told VH1.

Charles Hardin Holley was 22 years old when he died. Ritchie Valens was even younger, just 17. The 'La Bamba' star was as important to Mexican Americans and Latinos as Elvis was to white America. The Big Bopper, the dude who had the hit 'Chantilly Lace', was 28 years old. The deaths of those three young men moved so many people. It moved

Don McLean to write 'American Pie': 'I can't remember if I cried, When I read about his widowed bride, But something touched me deep inside, The day the music died.'

Buddy Holly was smart as a tack and one hell of a Rock 'n' Roll dude – he doesn't always get enough credit for it.

He grew up in Lubbock, Texas, the youngest of four children and nicknamed 'Buddy' by his mom. His parents weren't wealthy, but they insisted on music lessons for all their kids. Though Rock 'n' Roll was born out of kids rebelling against Ma and Pa, Holly's parents encouraged their son's musical inclinations. Buddy didn't quite cut it on the violin but his older brothers taught him a few guitar chords and a future Rock 'n' Roll star was born. In high school, he formed Buddy Holly and The Crickets (his surname was misspelt on a recording contract – 'Holly' instead of 'Holley'). They played Bluegrass and Country at local clubs, dances and talent shows.

After opening for Elvis in 1955, Holly begged his brother for the money to buy a Fender Strat. Country was out – Rock 'n' Roll was in. He started listening to more black music, a lot of R&B, and started hanging out at dances. Being in Texas and being the square-looking dude he was, it was very disarming. People wouldn't look at him and think, 'He's smoking dope and hanging out with black guys'. Later in his career, Buddy Holly and The Crickets were the first all-white band to play the Apollo Theater. Like Sinatra before him, Holly played a small part in challenging some of the perceptions of segregation.

In his all-too-brief career, Holly had hit after hit after hit. 'Peggy Sue' was inspired by drummer Jerry Allison's girlfriend (and later wife)

Peggy Sue Gerron. 'That'll Be the Day' was inspired by a John Wayne movie called *The Searchers*, in which Wayne often muttered, 'That'll be the day.' In later years, many people covered his songs; The Beatles did 'Words of Love', The Stones had a hit with 'Not Fade Away'. He had a huge influence on both bands, as well as on Elvis Costello and Bob Dylan, who in his 1998 Grammy acceptance speech talked about seeing Holly play when he was a teen. Holly was the nerdy kid to Elvis Presley's cool dude; he was a regular-looking guy playing extraordinary music.

Keith Richards talked about the Blues being based on improvisation; you're not going to see too much if you look at a Blues score. If you look at Buddy Holly's music, it's not that complicated either. It was simplistic, it wasn't overthought or overplayed. He cut right through any bullshit. He was making 2-minute 25-second songs with The Crickets; the perfect Pop song. Simplicity in music, when you get it right, is great. There's something to be said for being able to sing a simple song really fucking well. Buddy knew the market he was going for: the teenyboppers were coming up in spades and he had that vulnerable look that girls found adorable. He looked like a nerd, he played like a nerd – if there wasn't Buddy Holly there would be no Weezer – but he was actually very personable and knew how to handle himself.

Buddy was singing the Blues, but his version of it. It was the same chord progression and eight times out of ten it was the same subject matter. He was a true all-rounder, like Miles, like JB: bandleader, producer, arranger, writer, singer and player, and by all accounts a really nice fuckin' dude.

'To be a star, you obviously need a desirable amount of talent, but the most important factor is individuality – and Buddy was distinctive and unmistakable, both visually and aurally,' Frank Allen of The Searchers told the *Independent* in 2009. 'He looked gangly and geekish with those glasses but that guitar made him unbelievably cool, and he knew how to play it. It was the revenge of the nerd.'

*

SOUL POWER

Magnetism is a quality that comes up a lot when talking about great musicians; sexuality and charisma were definitely a big part of why many of these Rock 'n' Rollers were so popular with audiences. People were drawn to these singers and guitarists and drummers in ways that naturally occur between men and women, and women and women, and men and men. That's why we talk about these guys, because there was something about them that managed to be *other* from regular human beings.

The voice and the talent is one thing, but with someone like Otis Redding, this incredible presence was a huge part of his success. Otis had that magnetism by the truckload. That's what makes him special, legendary and an icon.

Otis was my man, he was like six foot something and 200-odd pounds – he was a *big* dude with an even bigger voice. He'd just knock you off your feet. Otis was just giving it to you straight raw, like the Wu-Tang Clan. He'd come out on stage holding a microphone and it would disappear in his hand, like a lighter does.

When Redding died at the age of 26, he was actually, in some ways, just getting started. Raised in the same town as Little Richard – Macon, Georgia – Redding took great influence from the 'Long Tall Sally' singer. 'If it weren't for Little Richard, I wouldn't be here,' Redding once said. 'I entered the music business because of Richard – he is my inspiration. I used to sing like Little Richard, his Rock 'n' Roll stuff... Richard has Soul too. My present music has a lot of him in it.'

From a really young age, Redding sung in a Gospel group and played drums in the school band. When his dad got sick, Otis, then 15, quit school to help support the family, working in a gas station, digging wells and performing with Little Richard's old group, The Upsetters. He won Macon's Sunday night talent show 15 weeks in a row and one day just drove on out to Memphis to begin his recording career. His big break came in 1962 with 'These Arms of Mine', which sold 800,000 copies on release. He was snapped up by Stax and released a volley of incredible, heart-aching Soul music: 'Try a Little Tenderness', 'Knock on Wood' (an Eddie Floyd cover he recorded with Carla Thomas), 'Respect' (later covered by Aretha), 'I've Been Loving You Too Long' – written in a hotel room over a bottle of J&B – and his version of The Stones' 'Satisfaction'.

Redding was Stax's most successful artist and was one of the first Soul artists to cross over to a white audience. In a deliberate attempt to reach that crowd, Redding decided to play at the Whisky a Go Go on LA's Sunset Strip in 1966 – the buzz was so big that even Bob Dylan showed up. In 1967, Redding crossed the Atlantic to Europe, winning the hearts of the UK, replacing Elvis Presley as the *Melody Maker's* Number One Male Vocalist. He returned home to play a set at the infamous Monterey Pop Festival alongside an almost exclusively white line-up that included The Mamas & the Papas, The Who and Janis Joplin. Jimi Hendrix and Brian Jones were said to be standing side of stage, rapt by Redding's performance. It was a performance from a man at the pinnacle of his career.

'I've never seen Otis so excited or proud,' said his wife, Zelma. 'He knew he had reached an audience he had never been able to reach before. Monterey Pop left Otis with such a great feeling about his career. He realized it was going to take him into another phase. He told me, "It's gonna put my career up some more right away."'

Six months later, however, he was dead.

Redding's death came shortly after the recording of his first proper crossover hit, '(Sittin' On) The Dock of the Bay', the lyrics of which were written on a houseboat in Sausalito. Purposefully trying to channel The Beatles' *Sgt Pepper's...*, Otis told his manager, Phil Walden, he'd written his first 'million-seller'. Four days later, on 10 December 1967, Redding and Stax's studio band, The Bar-Kays, chartered Otis's own plane, a Beechcraft H-18, from Cleveland to Wisconsin to play a show. Just four miles from Wisconsin as they came into land, the plane hit a fog-smothered Lake Monona and the plane was plunged into the lake's icy depths. In his autobiography, *The Godfather of Soul*, James Brown, from whom Redding had bought the plane, claimed to have told Otis not to use the aircraft with so much on board or in bad weather.

There was one survivor of the crash: Bar-Kays trumpeter Ben Cauley, who had awoken just before impact, undone his belt and grabbed on to a seat cushion. He couldn't swim, but he was able to stay afloat while the others were dragged down with the plane.

Redding, who was married with three children, received a star-studded send-off, with over 4,500 mourners in attendance at his funeral, including James Brown and Wilson Pickett. Booker T played the organ, and producer Jerry Wexler delivered the eulogy. In his 1993 autobiography, *Rhythm and the Blues*, Wexler said of Redding:

> *There was something pure about his personality, calm, dignified, vibrant... Stardom never changed him. He had a strong inner life. He was emotionally centered... Redding was one of those rare souls who saw beyond color and externalities; he dealt with you as a human being, not as white or black or a Christian or a Jew. His intelligence was keen, his curiosity high, and despite stories to the contrary he was anything but the cliché of the backwoods boy come to the big city. Otis knew what was happening.*

Otis got on the plane. He got on that plane, man. And when he did, it was the day that Soul music died.

*

HE AIN'T HEAVY

When Wilson Pickett rocked up in 1968 to Rick Hall's FAME Studio in Muscle Shoals, Alabama, he met a scrawny, white hairy kid clutching a guitar: Duane Allman. They hit it off right away. Pickett gave Allman his nickname 'Skydog', though the story differs as to why; it's either said to be due to his soaring guitar skills, or his reputation for getting high.

Back then, before The Allman Brothers formed, Duane was a struggling session musician living in the shadow of his more successful brother, Gregg. He had persuaded a reluctant Rick Hall to let him hang out at Shoals, and impressed him at sessions with the Blues and Soul singer Clarence Carter. The day Pickett showed up unannounced, Hall had no idea what track he should record. It was Allman who suggested 'Hey Jude' by The Beatles. Pickett and Hall scoffed at the idea of taking on such a huge band, until Allman pointed out the effect it could have. *Skydog: The Duane Allman Story* by Randy Poe describes Allman saying, 'The fact we cut the song with a black artist will get so much attention, it'll be an automatic smash.'

There's so much soul in that version, so much heart. Then you hear this guitar player come in for the solo and you can hear Allman telling Wilson that he belongs in that fucking room. It's a great song and a great energy.

'I remember hearing "Hey Jude" by Wilson Pickett and calling either Ahmet Ertegün or Tom Dowd and saying, "Who's that guitar player?",' said Eric Clapton of Allman's playing on the record. 'To this day, I've never heard better Rock guitar playing on an R&B record. It's the best.' Allman, who later became pals and played with Clapton, could be heard on a number of R&B tracks. His Blues-soaked playing on Aretha Franklin's 'The Weight', also recorded at Shoals, is sublime, while the classic riff Allman's slide recreates on Derek and the Dominos' 'Layla' tops even Clapton's version.

There was Jimi Hendrix and then there was Duane Allman. People use them as waypoints in guitar playing. We lost Hendrix and then we lost Duane Allman, at the age of 24.

The Allman Brothers was one of the biggest Rock 'n' Roll bands in the world at the time he died. They mixed it up with Blues, Country and Rock; you had the Blues progressions with the Country twang and the Rock 'n' Roll backbeat that was really going on at the time. They were selling out American football arenas – that was the birth of Arena Rock. Everyone was going out and making a big thing of it because Americans love going out to stadiums and tailgating, drinking a few beers. The Allman Brothers had a lot of great tracks; there's a lot of anthems, like 'Whipping Post', and they did some great guitar playing that paved the way for groups like Boston. They had their own fuzzed-out guitar sound. People were being so innovative in that era.

Duane liked his liquor and the harder drugs too, but, hey, he's in one of the biggest bands in the world. Let him enjoy himself. At the time he had his motorbike crash, he was said to have straightened out a bit. The group had just released *At Fillmore East*, which is still considered one of the best live albums ever recorded. A few months later, in October 1971, Duane was in Macon, Georgia (the home of Little Richard and Otis Redding), when he swerved his Harley-Davidson to avoid a truck. He hit the truck and was thrown clean from his bike; when he landed, his bike landed on top of him and he died from massive internal injuries.

He was one of those losses that people – and music – really felt.

✳

CRAZY IN LOVE

Patsy Cline should have known better than to get on a plane. She was a pretty big star; she'd just scored a nationwide hit with 'Crazy', written by a then-unknown Willie Nelson. She was, by all accounts, happily married with a couple of kids.

The plane, a Piper PA-24 Comanche, owned and flown by her manager, Randy Hughes, was dubbed 'The Shitbox' by her tour mates. Why would she get in somebody's private plane, let alone her manager's? Most managers are crazier than the damn artists! Add to that poor weather conditions that have already prevented you from taking off the day before, it's windy as hell and you're a musician. Don't get in the small plane! The Comanche was brought down by a mixture of inexperienced piloting and inclement weather, around 6.20pm on 5 March 1963.

Patsy was 30 when she died. She was the first female Country star thanks to hits like 'Walkin' After Midnight', 'She's Got You' and, of course, 'Crazy'. She was also the first female Country star to receive top billing over the male stars she was on tour with. And she was a tough cookie too; she was known to hang with the boys, swearing, drinking and calling them all 'Hoss'. She referred to herself as 'The Cline' and refused to go on stage until she'd been paid. 'No dough, no show' was one of her catchphrases. She was supportive of other women too, helping the likes of Loretta Lynn in her own Country career. 'When Patsy died, my God, not only did I lose my best girlfriend, but I lost a great person that was taking care of me. I thought, now somebody will whip me for sure,' Lynn later told *Entertainment Weekly*.

She was a tough but she had a warm heart; after a dramatic car crash in which she was thrown through the windshield, Cline insisted the paramedics attend to the female driver of the other vehicle first.

Cline grew up poor; I guess that's where that voice came from. Pain and suffering never did hurt a pair of pipes too much. Her ma was 16 and her pops 43 when she was born in Winchester, Virginia, in 1932. For Cline's first couple of years, the family lived in a cabin without water or electricity. Later on, her dad landed a job as a boilerman for Washington and Lee University, and the family moved to the relative luxury of a house in the woods near the campus. Her dad eventually left home, so as a teen Patsy worked a number of jobs to help provide; there were shifts in an abattoir, a movie snack bar and at a drugstore. She would be out in bars singing Country music – none too popular back then in a provincial town like Winchester. Cline must have cut quite a figure back in the Forties and Fifties: deadbeat dad, divorced mother, singing about broken hearts, and drinking beer and wearing trousers.

Patsy Cline always did things her way and I guess that would be her undoing. Her friend Dottie West, wary of Cline flying in potentially bad weather, had offered her a ride from Kansas – where she'd been performing at a benefit for a DJ who had died in a car crash – back to her Nashville home. But Patsy, anxious to get back to her husband and kids, said she'd jump on a flight. 'Don't worry about me, Hoss. When it's my time to go, it's my time to go.' A week earlier, referring to her two previous car crashes, she had apparently told a backing singer that the next time would be third time lucky – or unlucky. 'I've had two bad ones.

[Next time] will either be a charm or it'll kill me.'

This attitude was echoed nearly 40 years later by TLC's Lisa 'Left Eye' Lopes, who had often talked about the premonitions she'd had about dying at a young age. A few days before her death, also at the age of 30, Lopes had been a passenger in a car that had accidentally run down a ten-year-old boy whose surname was Lopez. She was said to have believed the spirits were after her but had taken the boy by mistake. Two weeks later, she died of neck injuries and severe head trauma following a crash in Honduras.

I guess Left Eye and Patsy just hit it out of the park. Patsy said, 'I'm gonna hit that ball right over there in that corner.' And then: boom. She probably had a kind of Spidey-sense that the crash was going to happen. You don't say things like those girls said flippantly.

Patsy Cline did a Babe Ruth. She pointed to where she was gonna hit the home run and then she fuckin' hit it.

*

WE WERE GIVEN A QUEEN

Aaliyah was Beyoncé squared, on every level. A better singer, a better actress, a better dancer… Beyoncé is great and everything, but Aaliyah had a sensitivity and vulnerability and a sincerity that is somehow lacking in Beyoncé and a lot of these stars right now. She contributed so much to music in such a short period of time, and was just about to do what Pasty Cline was just about to do, what Jeff Buckley was just about to do, what Shannon Hoon was just about to do. Sometimes it seems almost inevitable that something so powerful upsets the natural flow of the universe and has to be quickly dismantled. We can't have these extremes because whenever we have these extremes, things start getting out of the natural selection and order. So they have to go.

Aaliyah had had a crazy life before she'd even turned 16. She was signed at 12, allegedly illegally married at 15 to R Kelly (though both parties denied the marriage) – probably one of the freakiest freaks we've ever seen in music – and a star that same year with her debut album, *Age Ain't Nothing but a Number*. She worked with two of Hip-Hop's most innovative sound sculptors – Missy Elliott and Timbaland – and won roles in a number of movies including *The Matrix*. She was slated for four movies before she passed away. She was dead by 22.

One of my oldest friends in the world, Derek Lee, was Aaliyah's stylist. I've been friends with him since I was a kid; his mom and my mom were friends. He was with Aaliyah in the Bahamas, where she died. They were there to shoot a video for 'Rock the Boat'. The shoot had finished a day early and Aaliyah had invited Derek to jump on the plane and go with her to Miami to hang out. He decided to fly back to New York instead, but drove out to the airport with her. Aaliyah and eight others – including the pilot – boarded the twin-engine Cessna 402B at Marsh Harbour airport. It was smaller than the Cessna they had arrived on, but was loaded with the same amount of luggage. The plane crashed almost immediately – 200 feet from the end of the runway. It was Derek who had to go and identify the bodies, because he knew everyone on the plane. At the autopsy, the pilot, Luis Morales III, was found to have cocaine and alcohol in his system. A fucked-up pilot and an overloaded Cessna aren't ideal conditions for flying.

The inscription on Aaliyah's portrait at the funeral read: 'We Were Given a Queen, We Were Given an Angel'.

On the surface, with her Tommy Hilfiger's hanging low, ubiquitous shades and stomping Timberland boots, Aaliyah came across as a mean-ass street diva, but she was the sweetest girl in the world, by all accounts. She would go out with cash on her – or her bodyguard would – and she'd give homeless guys hundred-dollar bills. 'Street but sweet' is how she described her music. Her innovative approach to music reached far outside the worlds of R&B and Hip-Hop; everyone from Adele and The xx have noted Aaliyah's influence on their work.

I began this chapter with the death of a 22-year-old on a privately chartered plane, and I also end it with the death of a 22-year-old on a privately chartered plane. We'll never know where any of these greats might have taken music. We've lost too many before their time, people who could still have been contributing positively to music today and maybe changing the way things are. Imagine if Dylan had died before he cut 'The Times They Are a-Changin'', or Richards had checked out pre-'Exile on Main St'. We can't know and we'll never know, but one thing is for certain: planes and Pop stars do not a good mix make.

WHILE MY GUITAR GENTLY WEEPS

The electric guitar set a lot of people free. When you get down to it, it's just wood, plastic and metal, but in the right hands it can be a lifesaver – for the people who play it as well as the people who listen to it.

It's the symbol of Rock 'n' Roll, or popular music, or whatever we want to call it. It was in every band pretty much up until the Eighties, when bands became synthesizer-based for a while. But they came back to it. The guitar is everywhere again now; just look at Mark Ronson's 'Uptown Funk', or bands like Royal Blood and The Staves. There are guitars in Hip-Hop, even though you might not associate the two; there were a lot of Blues guitars in many of the popular Hip-Hop breaks, like Billy Squier's 'The Big Beat' and Incredible Bongo Band's cover of The Shadows' track 'Apache'. They were always intertwined but I don't know if they knew it. It's kinda like holding hands with a stranger in the dark. They were walking in the dark trying to find the light together.

The evolution of the guitar came with amplification. They plugged it in and suddenly it could replace the sonic frequencies of the horn section; now you could play different chords or hit different notes and the music didn't feel depleted. Then there were great guitar players in the Jazz era: Wes Montgomery really pushed boundaries with the guitar. He was known as one of the great innovators and improvisers of guitar, a self-taught musician who used his thumb as a pick, which was really unorthodox, but gave his playing this really awesome, soft, delicate sound. He also developed the idea of playing in octaves – the same note on two strings, an octave apart – which had previously been thought impossible. Montgomery, a father of seven who worked three jobs until finally finding success in his mid-thirties, died of a heart attack at the peak of his success when he was 45 years old.

We all know about the Delta Blues guys, playing acoustic instruments, but when they left the South to head up to Chicago, the Electric Blues was born.

*

STILL WATERS RUN DEEP

Blues guitarists were – and are – so important because when you look back to the past, you might find something that will lead you into the future. You're looking for a key, and with guitar players, they're constantly reinventing the wheel. It's the way in which people use their whole being to play that guitar as an instrument to express themselves. It wouldn't be Rock 'n' Roll without the electric guitar; that was the tool that allowed it to happen. Playing the piano loudly wouldn't have done it. We needed the guitar to get amplified in order for Led Zeppelin, Jimi Hendrix and The Stones to exist. One of the greats of Electric Blues, and a man who influenced all of the above, was McKinley Morganfield, aka Muddy Waters, born in Mississippi in 1913.

Muddy Waters was the Father of the Electric Blues. He was another guy who was almost sidelined when the Blues' popularity declined; we almost didn't get 1968's *Electric Mud*, which is one of the greatest Blues albums ever. Thankfully, the use of Blues in Rock 'n' Roll ensured a resurgence in the scene, and dudes like Muddy got another crack at the whip. Producer Marshall Chess – the son of the founder of Chess Records – pretty much resurrected Waters's career by effectively going, 'Hey, Muddy, let's make a record that's all your best Electric Blues from back in the day, and record it now, in 1968, with a multi-track studio, and make it for real.' *Electric Mud* became controversial for its use of eccentric psychedelia, but it went on to influence everyone from Hendrix to John Paul Jones and, in later years, even Public Enemy's Chuck D. It's even considered a precursor of Hip-Hop. It's seminal. If you don't have *Electric Mud* in your record collection, you don't have a Blues record collection. If you're a person who enjoys Blues music, you have to have heard of *Electric Mud*; if you haven't, get out there and buy it. It's Muddy Waters electrified in the year 1968, but with everybody appreciating what he fucking did in the Forties and Fifties.

Muddy's career suffered in the Sixties – no one was paying attention – but then the Blues got another shot at it, because people like Jimi Hendrix and The Stones began paying it so much attention. Albert King supported Jimi Hendrix on tour, Led Zeppelin covered 'Blind' Willie Johnson, and later on you had Keith Richards doing that Chuck Berry movie, *Hail! Hail! Rock 'n' Roll*, which is hilarious just for that one bit where Keith says of Chuck Berry, 'He's the only guy who hit me in the face who I didn't hit back.'

Once you had guys who were selling millions of records that borrowed so greatly from the Blues, suddenly these old Blues men found they had an audience all over again. And Muddy was one of the most popular. 'The first guitar player I was aware of was Muddy Waters,' Hendrix said. 'I first heard him as a little boy and it scared me to death.'

Waters was the man who put Chess Records on the map in 1948 with his single 'I Can't Be Satisfied', regarded as a masterpiece in Electric Blues recording. In 1958 he headed over to England, where he shocked audiences with the volume of his amplified guitar; until then, they'd only heard acoustic Folk or Blues. He plugged it in and turned it up high – real high. He was such an influential figure. Muddy, and a lot of his peers, became really big in Europe, where crowds were known to be more open to experimentation than in the US. In '58, you had Rockabilly and Elvis, where the white man was playing the Blues, so a lot of the black musicians were sidelined and had to look for somewhere else to go. A lot of them went to Europe – a lot of Jazz dudes went to Paris and London around the same time. They were appreciated in Europe; they could make money there. They influenced whole generations of musicians that way who were keen to dig into the history of the Blues and discover the greats.

In 1964, on their first tour of the US, The Stones made a pilgrimage to 2120 South Michigan Avenue, Chicago, home of Chess Records and artists including Waters, Howlin' Wolf, Chuck Berry and Bo

Diddley. Inspired by being in the hallowed four walls of the studio, they recorded 14 tracks in two days, including their first number one, 'It's All Over Now'.

'They went, "Ah, man, I don't believe it, you're playing our music",' Keith Richards told BBC4's *Blues Britannia* programme of the reaction of the Blues men to a ragtag bunch of Londoners turning up at their door. 'They were just so effusive, so sweet – "Come over to the house", you know. I mean, you'd died and gone to heaven – it was the cats, gentlemen in the truest sense of the term... They were so interested in what we were doing, and realizing, at the same time, that we didn't know shit, really. They would all help; it was all encouragement, and that. To me, that was one of the most heartwarming things. Because you figure you're gonna walk in [and they'd think], "Snooty little English guys and a couple of hit records." Not at all. I got the chance to sit around with Muddy Waters and Bobby Womack, and they just wanted to share ideas... They wanted to know how we were doing it, and why we wanted to do it, you know.'

Muddy Waters is the man who plugged the Blues in; and once the Blues got electrified, there was no stopping it. That's why we see those big 'ole branches in Rock 'n' Roll and Hip-Hop and Punk and even Disco. The live album, *At Newport 1960*, solidified his status as King of the Blues, but Chess put him on a backburner until he teamed up with Diddley, Little Walter and Howlin' Wolf to record *Super Blues*. *Electric Mud* followed the year after. 'Rolling Stone' was one of his big tunes – both the band and the magazine nodded towards that track. You had everyone from Led Zeppelin to Cream, The Allman Brothers and AC/

DC covering Waters. You can barely watch a Scorsese film without hearing Waters as De Niro beats some poor schmuck to death.

Rock 'n' Roll was coined by Blues musicians and adopted by the new generation of musicians playing 12-bar Blues. Keith Richards told me, 'If you look at it written down on paper, on sheet music, it don't look like much. But it's all in the heart and how you play it and express yourself in those 12 bars.' And when Muddy played the Blues, he played it like no other.

*

SONIC EXPERIMENTS

The Electric Blues showed how, if you start turning an amp up, the tubes start to distort and those old amps sound really rattled and cool. Some dudes turned their amps up all the way, and from there it's obvious from the sonics and the physics of it how you could create certain sounds with gain and tones that you wouldn't have imagined possible before. It became a battle of the tones. You know the second Brian May picks up a guitar, because he created a tone for himself; same with Jimmy Page and Eric Clapton. Eric Clapton has had a lot of setbacks in his life and pissed off a lot of people, but he broke so much ground with Cream. Jack Bruce too. Those two guys are the curators of the Blues who took the guitar to the psychedelic level in the mid-Sixties.

You have guys like Duane Allman and Jimi Hendrix and Rory Gallagher who were hard-living dudes. If you listen to Rory Gallagher's recordings, he was so on the one, despite apparently being a chronic alcoholic. The recordings I've heard are amazing; he was so different from everyone else. This cat was really a charming, awesome entertainer who sold mad numbers of records – tens of millions worldwide. Born in Donegal and raised in Cork, he was a craftsman of the Blues and was looked up to by all the greats including Jimi, Jimmy Page and Keith. His band, Taste, was blisteringly great and he deservedly got a rep for slaying it live. There's an urban myth, never fully substantiated, but apparently Jimi Hendrix was once asked how it felt to be the best guitarist in the world, 'I don't know. Ask Rory Gallagher,' he replied. He was a true purist who refused to sell out his sound and only ever released albums because he saw how the singles market was diluting everything for proper musicians.

I have a reproduction of his '61 Stratocaster and I play better when I'm using it, for real.

He was so freaked about flying that he took pills and drank on them and that shit killed him at the age of 47; he died from taking sedatives so that he could continue to do gigs for his fans. Renegade shit, bad logic.

He played the Blues better than most other musicians did, but he didn't have the longevity to make his name a household one, although most cats know him if they play geetar or know about Electric Blues.

I first heard about him when I was serving with the Marines. A buddy of mine was a bootleg junkie and had this tape of him playing somewhere down south. I could not stop listening to it so, in the end, my bro gave me the cassette and made me buy him a pitcher of beer at the enlisted club on base.

Rory was playing the Blues just as well as Hendrix, in his way.

Gallagher was more of a traditionalist than Hendrix; he was fine art and Jimi was an Impressionist. Look at the Beat poets of the Sixties, like Ginsberg: those guys were trying to do different things with sound and change things people considered to be normal. That's what was going on in the Sixties – a social revolution was happening, which included the Civil Rights Movement but also the way people looked at their lives. In the decades after World War II, people started thinking everything was hunky-dory so they'd go out drinking and there would be music and sounds made people happy. It's a bit like our post-recession times, with people getting so into Pharrell's 'Happy'!

That's what brought people into loving music and how it became central to their lives, in some cases. Music is certainly central to my life. I constantly listen to music – all types of music. I can't stop listening to music because it would lessen the emotions I feel in life, good or bad. It would diminish life in general if there were no music. That's how I feel about it.

When you want to differentiate between guitarists, it comes down to approach and personality. They gave Clapton the nickname 'Slowhand' for a reason. He'd rock out when he had to but he didn't do any trickery. His playing is awesome, and he does play fast, but every note meant something. Like B B King. They made records together because they found that similarity in each other. The difference between him and Jimmy Page is that Page is aggressively playing the Blues – the Electric Blues. Page is considered up there with the greats; he really set the tone and mood for those nine Led Zep studio records. Before setting up the band with Plant, John Bonham and John Paul Jones, Page was the go-to guy in the Sixties, playing with The Kinks, The Yardbirds, The Everly Brothers and Nico.

It also comes down to the people these guitar greats were playing with. The ones we're talking about chose to play with incredible singers and musicians: Richards and Jagger, Page and Plant, Hendrix and the guys he played with in the Experience and on *Band of Gypsys*.

When all the English guys like Richards and McCartney saw Hendrix, they were like, 'Where do we go now?' It wasn't Rock 'n' Roll, it wasn't Funk – it was something else. Then, after *Sgt Pepper's* people were looking for another way to be different and so Hendrix and Allman and all those other musicians came through. A lot of times Hendrix pushed it so much that you could barely tell it was the guitar he was playing. Check out 'Bold as Love' on YouTube. It's Jimi trying out guitar sounds with the band before they do the take. You can hear him feeling his way through the whole sonicsphere. It's like Jimi exploring space. That's what he was doing, really: exploring space. He could go in any direction; it's infinite. That's the one thing about the guitar: its continuous evolution. Even through the whole synthesizer era, there was a guitar in every video somewhere because it was a symbol of something that was rebellious; it was loud and bratty, to a certain extent. When Punk Rock came along, everyone picked up the guitar and learnt four chords, but then the cream rose to the top and we had Joe Strummer and The Clash.

That's the great thing about that music back then: it came from the heart and it was modern-day Blues. And it crept in everywhere. It happened with a lot of R&B stuff, like 'Wild Little Tiger' by The Isley

Brothers with Jimi Hendrix. That song is a great example of how way-out-there Jimi was. The song was out-there to begin with, but then Jimi starts playing a solo and it's even clearer how ahead of their time these guys were. He was always doing that – pushing people.

Next you have to listen to 'Clash City Rockers', a Clash single from '78. I bought it the day it came out. And that opening riff is mind-blowing. The guitar was so bratty and snotty-sounding, but then it led into some really virtuoso playing by Mick Jones, which was a throwback to old Rock, in a way. Their feet were half in the old and half in the new, and then they came fully into the new when they merged it with Hip-Hop. A little later you see how the guitar crept into early Run DMC, produced by Rick Rubin (a guitar player himself), which evolved into the Beastie Boys, who were a Punk band that played the guitar – Kerry King from Slayer played on 'No Sleep till Brooklyn'. When records like that came out it was like an atomic bomb dropping – songs like that blew everything else out of their path: that sound of rebellion.

*

ONE-MINUTE MAN

Over on the other side of the Atlantic, D Boon was a hugely influential figure in American Punk Rock. He's another member of that infamous 27 Club: Boon died in a van accident in 1985. A real tragic accident. He'd been sick and was in the back of the van, lying down, without a seatbelt. His girlfriend, who was driving, ran the vehicle off the road and Boon was thrown out of the back. He broke his neck and died instantly.

He didn't get a whole lot of limelight but he should have. Though he wasn't around for long, he changed the way people approached the guitar. D Boon used a lot of distortion and equalization and referenced heavy Funk, Jazz and Folk. *Rolling Stone* described Minutemen's seminal album *Double Nickels* on the Dime as venturing 'thrillingly into free-jazz dissonance, up-tempo country, helter-skelter funk and dense experimental rock'. He was a political dude too; his songs were about the working classes and The Man.

Having been in a band for as long as I have, every time I play the same song I play it differently – just because it's a different time and space. That's what Boon did and he did a great job of it. It was next-level shit; he made you look at the guitar all over again. He was a guy trying to do something different.

He was in two bands: The Reactionaries and later the Californian Punk band, Minutemen. Minutemen – which was founded by Boon and his childhood buddy Mike Watt – called their style 'Econo Rock', meaning that they did everything as cheaply and sparsely as possible. They were truly DIY. They were a band about touring, not recording, though they put out a hell of a lot of records in a short time. They only used records as a way to get booked for gigs. Hence they made their music as cheaply as possible, but their style was economical too.

'To me, the high point is *Double Nickels*. Some of those guitar solos D Boon does on "Anxious Mofo" and "June 16th" are so econo, choosin' very few notes,' Mike Watt told the *Village Voice* in 2011. 'It's really intense… D Boon played… gig[s]… like the whole world depended on it. I loved it.'

There's a great book about Minutemen by Michael Azerrad, based on the lyrics to one of their songs, *Our Band Could Be Your Life*, and in 2005 a documentary by Tim Irwin and Keith Schieron came out called *We Jam Econo*, based on their recording techniques. It's testament to their influence that everyone from Thurston Moore to Henry Rollins and Flea is in the film.

'What we try to do is change our music and change people's ideas, maybe reaching a larger audience, without selling out. All this is kind of hit and miss, but I love it,' said Boon back in 1985, in an interview with the fanzine *Suburban Voice*.

He was one of the most Punk Rock guitarists of all time and Minutemen are one of the most influential American Punk Rock bands of all time. He was truly a star that burned briefly but burned bright.

It's a good thing a lot of them are still with us, like Jimmy Page and Jeff Beck, but the ones we lost were the ones that were really taking us places. Stevie Ray Vaughan, for example. Don't get on the chopper, dude, you're a great musician! He brought Hendrix back, almost, because he was so beholden to that style of Blues. He did his own covers of Hendrix songs, he did them brilliantly, but he did them his own way. He played homage, but very much retained his own sensibilities. In the mid-Eighties, when he played on David Bowie's 'Let's Dance', produced by Nile Rodgers, that's when guitar started to come back to the mainstream.

*

THE HITMAKER

Nile Rodgers is responsible for guitar being in R&B and Funk and Pop to this day. He's constantly reinventing how people are hearing and using guitar. There's a five-minute guitar solo called 'Savoir Faire' on Chic's 1978 album *C'est Chic*, the biggest-selling Disco record of its generation – 'Le Freak' and 'Chic Cheer' were both on it. That was a record that got me knowing how to play – and how not to play – guitar. I'm glad that we have those people around today, still kicking it. Nile played with Daft Punk and made them sound like Chic! He didn't reinvent the wheel; he just did what he did and Daft Punk got cool with it.

Nile's contribution can't be overstated. He got a gig on the *Sesame Street* band before forming Chic, and went on to write for Diana Ross and Robert Plant. In the Eighties, and beyond, he produced massive hits, including 'Like a Virgin', 'The Reflex', 'Let's Dance', and 'We Are Family', and of course 2013's 'Get Lucky' (the latter two he co-wrote), not to mention all of those Chic hits. He's sold over 100 million albums during his six decades in the game; his discography is ridiculous.

He let me hold the Hitmaker once – it's a customized Strat: a 1960 body with a '59 neck that he picked up many years ago in a shop in Miami Beach. It's the one he's written all the hits on, and according to him it doesn't sound like any other Stratocaster in the world. It's been valued at £1.3 billion because of the number of hits he's written on it.

I got chatting to Nile on Twitter and it turned out he was a fan of the Criminals. When I was in New York to do a radio documentary, he agreed to be on it, so we went and hung out at his place for a few hours, talking about music. He has the whole floor in a beautiful old baroque building in New York. It's massive. He grew up in the city, like me. He said when his parents were doing good they'd be in the Village, but when they weren't it was over to Alphabet City and the South Bronx! He grew up listening to all types of music too and because of that he's flirted with so many genres. Like I was saying earlier, the guitar could even be found in Hip-Hop; one of the best examples has to be Grandmaster Flash and the Furious Five sampling Nile's riff from 'Good Times' in 'Rapper's Delight'. That record in itself is seminal; it was the track that introduced Hip-Hop to the world.

I imagine because he's so well known as a Pop and Disco hitmaker that Rodger's technique is overlooked. But he's an incredibly proficient, talented player. 'The right hand and the left hand are almost married when I play,' he says.

Nile Rodgers only took up the guitar in the first place to impress a girl. I don't know who that chick was, but I'm sure as hell glad that Nile met her.

*

THE LEGACY

It seems a shame that there's no scene for these kids anymore. I listen to Gary Clark Jr play – he's the next guy in the Blues scene. He's played on stage with The Stones and he's opened up for Eric Clapton at the Royal Albert Hall. He blew Clapton off the stage. But who does he get to play beside, bounce ideas off, jam with? There would be a community in the LA scene where Crosby, Stills, Nash, Neil Young, Jackson Browne, Linda Ronstadt all hung out together and wrote songs for each other. In New York, you had David Bowie, David Byrne, Blondie, The Velvet Underground and the downtown scene with Richard Hell and Johnny Thunders. It was a community of musicians. Throughout all that, the guitar was always there.

The guitar is the backbone of the band, as integral as drums or the lead vocalist. In a lot of cases, the guitarist has always tended to be the wildest one in the band. When you don't have to take care of your instrument of expression – like your voice – then you can afford to be a little crazier. As a singer, there are only so many times you can get fucked up and lose your voice before people stop booking you. As a guitar player, you don't have that restriction. If you're of Rock star status and you don't have to show up for the vocal coach or the TV interviews, you can go crazy. That's why a lot of these guitar players have crazier reputations than the singer.

I chose the guitar because it has a sound that haunted me – still does. The guitar can take you off the ledge; it can put you on the ledge; it can throw you off the ledge. But, for most of us, the guitar is a saviour. You show someone a picture of Les Paul or a Strat and they'll say 'Rock 'n' Roll'. It's a symbol of rebellion.

KEEPING THE FLAME BURNING

Rock 'n' Roll was ruined by the things that we thought would make our society better: the Internet, 360-degree media coverage, living a more wholesome, considered life. Rock 'n' Roll can't be Rock 'n' Roll now because we've built a society where Rock 'n' Roll no longer has a place. Everyone now is more interested in making money than in making music. And that's the problem: it was always the music business but now it's *just* business. Money changes everything and everybody. It removes all willingness to take a risk, to put your balls on the table, to be crazy and blow up your drums, to take loads of acid and play 'The Star-Spangled Banner' on stage in front of 100,000 people, or risk being arrested or deported for writing a protest song. People perceive there to be so much at stake – financially – that they're not prepared to take a chance and create something for pure creative and spiritual gain.

I started this book by saying that Rock 'n' Roll died when Kurt Cobain killed himself. And as a driving force in music it truly did. But there are musicians who have kept the embers stoked, despite a ton of cold water being poured on them.

We all think we know Kurt Cobain. He's the guy who made us stop and take notice, made us realize that being 'famous' was for suckers who had no talent; but he was a victim of his own ideals. When Nirvana burst on the scene it was painfully obvious that this band wasn't just some 'grunge' act from Seattle that was going to fade away as soon as the Seattle scene was co-opted by the major labels, and the fact was they didn't.

More and more people identified with Kurt and his battle with drugs and fame and a crazy-ass wife. Folks knew he wasn't full of shit and that really, really mattered. We saw and felt his pain and obvious confusion with the wordwide acclaim his band was getting; we almost wanted him to do or say something about it.

I get a feeling he had no fucking idea Nirvana was gonna blast the doors off of MTV and garner so much attention from people who, in his mind, had no damn idea where he was actually coming from. He didn't see this coming and when it was all up in his face, he had to try to deal with it. His bandmates were his best friends, his family, and they knew – as only a bandmate can – what he was going through in order to rationalize and come to terms with fame and becoming an icon overnight.

When I opened the book with Kurt's suicide being the point in which 'it' all stopped being real, I wasn't being sensational about it. Just think of what's happened since then. I'm not propping him up without thinking about the facts; these are the facts.

Shit changed for the worse. I can cite hundreds of reasons for this, but when you talk about Kurt, or when I talk about Kurt; it's personal.

He was a person who wanted the abstract dream of playing his music for like-minded people, who had the same issues with the modern world he had. His lyrics and music spoke volumes and were a testament to why we loved it. All the crap in the world – war, poverty, racism, sexism, classism, drugs and the marginalization of an entire generation – was his burden.

As many great artists do, he felt things acutely. He couldn't turn on the TV and veg to some sitcom and sedate himself; he was too smart for that shit. And with that, artistic endeavours that came after him were no longer commercially viable because we could smell and see through the bullshit.

Kurt was just a dude who was extraordinarily talented and with this talent came a certain sensitivity that was exploited until he couldn't take it any more. His music will live on like all great music does, but when I listen to Nirvana, I'm reminded of the line by Hunter S Thompson in *Fear and Loathing in Las Vegas*, 'So now, less than five years later, you can go up on a steep hill in Las Vegas and look West, and with the right kind of eyes you can almost see the high-water mark – that place where the wave finally broke and rolled back.'

*

REDEMPTION SONG

Like many people, I thought having a black Democratic American president was going to bring about great change. I thought that it would open up the floodgates for people to be more political in their music.

Though that doesn't seem to have been the case, there are a couple who have struck a chord – artists like Atlanta-born Cody ChesnuTT, for example, whose 2012 album, *Landing on a Hundred,* is one of the best records to come out in recent times. What I love about Cody is that he invokes the past but it feels like the future. He made that record with a ten-piece band in Memphis, at Royal Studios, where Al Green, Ike and Tina and Buddy Guy have recorded.

'The original tracks were cut on two-inch tape. My hands were tingling, because I got to sing on the actual microphone that Al Green recorded with,' Cody explains on his official website. 'Nothing has changed. The down home acoustic treatments are still in place.'

Cody is one of those guys, like Johnny Cash, who was saved by becoming a family man. He'd put out his first album, *The Headphone Masterpiece,* in 2002 and it was this ambitious, lo-fi double album that he made in his bedroom. When he wrote it, he was having affairs with two women while being married to third, and that's where a lot of that first – I guess you could say libidinous – record came from! Once he sorted his shit out with his wife, though, they had a child and he became a family man. He lives in Tallahassee, Florida now and he's got a ride-on mower on which he thinks up his songs. Life is pretty simple and straightforward and it's unlocked a new level of creativity for him. He took some time out, and when he returned he had this great new record, *Landing on a Hundred.*

You find a place in your life that you're comfortable with, and if you're a music-maker, it makes your music better. It might not be commercially viable; I mean, I don't hear a lot of Cody's stuff on the radio – I play him, obviously – but in America he's known as the guy in the army helmet. He's still very political – wearing that helmet was his sign of being supportive. Like, 'It could be me out there in Afghanistan – what's the fucking difference? I'm just another black guy, and if I didn't have music I probably would have joined up too.' Because that's usually what happens. It's the poorest of the poor in our society who go off and fight the wars of the rich. And there's something to be said about that. I mean, in my records I address all that stuff. I know records that I make with themes along those lines are probably going to sell wood in the hood, but whatever it sells, it's an artistic endeavour. I'm trying to say something. That kind of stuff just doesn't fly nowadays.

I also like the record that The Roots did in 2010 with John Legend. It's called *Wake Up!*, and it is predominantly covers of protest songs from the Sixties and Seventies: Baby Huey's 'Hard Times', Bill Withers's 'I Can't Write Left Handed' and 'Wake Up Everybody' by Harold Melvin and the Blue Notes. It pretty much underscores everything I've said in this book; that the potency of these protest songs can't be overstated. They make as much sense and mean as much now as they did back in the days when they were first made. I also thought it was cool that John Legend and Common won the Oscar for 'Glory', taken from the movie *Selma*. I think that song did so well because it talks about the continuing struggle for civil rights in the US. It picks up on all the crazy shit that went down in the Fifties and Sixties and really elegantly points out that there's still a whole lot more to be done.

In writing this book, I did a search of records of meaning that have been released in the last year or so, and it's overwhelmingly rappers that have the most to say. Following Ferguson, we've seen guys like The Game, J Cole and Kendrick Lamar drop thought-proving records that delve a lot deeper than your average Taylor Swift or Iggy Azalea single. Pharoahe Monch recorded 'Stand Your Ground', following the acquittal of George Zimmerman. In 2014, Questlove, the drummer from the Roots, posted a lengthy Instagram plea to artists, seeking '... the new Dylans, new Public Enemys, new Nina Simones, new De La Rochas. I urge musicians and artists alike to push themselves to be a voice of the times that we live in. New ideas,' he railed. 'Real narratives. Songs with spirit in them. Songs with solutions. Songs with questions. Protest songs don't have to be boring or un-danceable or ready made for the next Olympics. They just have to speak the truth.'

Amen brother! It's down to us too, as fans, as consumers of music, to actively search these sounds out and pay for them. Stop listening to music on Spotify and buy a CD or an MP3 that isn't the same drivel force-fed to us. It's frustrating that records like the above aren't being heard more; it's crazy that most radio and newspapers give songs with something to say so little airplay and coverage.

When you look at people like Billie Holiday or Marvin Gaye or the band Buffalo Springfield, who released 'For What It's Worth', there were musicians out there who really stood up to protest against the injustices going on. And people wanted to hear it. So they went out and bought it. In their millions. But nowadays we don't have any of that because it's not palatable; record labels and radio stations have decided that people don't want to be reminded of death and destruction, even though it's going on, and it's creeping nearer to us every day.

There are kids now that have the experience of ten lifetimes to tell us about, who've lived through wars and all kinds of horror. Yet what we're being fed on the airwaves is so diluted and homogenized. There are people out there doing great things but when record labels are looking for Pop machines happy to churn out safe, predictable, sure-fire hits, what hope do they have of breaking through?

But there are going to be kids coming through. I have faith. Something's going to happen, probably from someplace that we're not even looking at. No one saw Cobain coming or Hendrix coming or The Beatles coming. The latter were a honky-tonk band who'd played a few shows in Germany. Then someone cut their hair all funny and they started singing, 'Yeah, Yeah, Yeah', and that was it. There are rappers coming through like Bishop Nehru, who's a kid from upstate New York. He's the type of artist who's going to make us realize what we've been missing. There's a bunch of kids like Spooky Black and Allan Kingdom making noise in Saint Paul, Minnesota. The Grime scene over in the UK seems to be having a great moment. I think Plan B is awesome – he's got that Rock 'n' Roll swagger to him. I'm looking forward to hearing whatever he has to say next.

I don't know if it will be Rock as a genre that will provide the next rebel hero, though. You have to stay in the box nowadays. The Milk are two brothers, a singer and a guitar player from Chelmsford, who are doing it for the love. They had a deal with Sony that they bought themselves out of so they could sign with Wah Wah 45s. They have a song called 'Favourite Worry' – it's so fucking amazing. But no one has really picked up on them yet, and I'm guessing that's because they're not four young, pretty, teenage boys.

Michael Kiwanuka's *Home Again* was produced as though it were 1974. So beautiful. But you didn't hear enough about this kid. Why? I guess because it's all mathematics and finances. His album wasn't a big seller, there were no 'radio-friendly hit singles'; he's singing some spiritual stuff on that record. That shit isn't going to get a huge push because he's not singing about tits and ass. I think Kiwanuka's off making another album and I hope he gets the support he needs so that people go out and buy it. How can we produce Marvins and Janises if we don't give these kids the time and space to develop and build an audience?

*

LONG MAY HIS PURPLE REIGN

A perfect example of an artist being given the time and space to develop his talent is Prince Rogers Nelson. He wrote his first song at seven years old and by 17 he was signed. His success was far from overnight. It took a few years and a good couple of albums before Prince became a global megastar. But he had confidence in himself from the off; when he got signed at 17, Prince cut himself a deal that meant he not only had full creative control, but that he also owned his own publishing rights.

I met Prince once, sometime around '93 or '94. I was a bar-back at this club, the Limelight, in Times Square, and Prince was throwing an afterparty. Before he showed up, the manager gave us all these rules and regulations. 'You can't talk to him or address him. Don't even look at him. Just stay the fuck away from him and if you're in his presence, just let him be, or he's gonna pull this thing and it will cost us a lot of money.' I was like, 'Whatever.' I wasn't a stagehand, I was a bar-back; I had no need to bother the guy. I carried ice around and brought beer to the dressing room. Hence how I came to meet him.

The manager told me, 'Bring beer to Prince's dressing room.' I was the head bar-back so I was like, 'I'm not bringing it. I don't want to get fired.' All the other kids were Mexican and they're like, 'They'll fire our asses faster than you, white boy', so I had to be the one to take the beers. I get a crate and push through the crowded club, through to the back behind the stage where the dressing rooms are. I knock on the door and I hear a quiet 'Hello.' I open the door and standing directly in the middle of the room is Prince. He's got his hands in his pockets and he's looking right at me. He's like, 'Hello.' I'm like, 'Hi. I have this beer for your band.' He's like, 'Set it down over there. If you want one, have one.' I'm like, 'Thank you, Prince, that's real nice. Have a good show, man, knock 'em dead.' I'd forgotten about this whole 'Don't talk to him' business because he was just a nice, normal guy, totally cool.

So that's that. I go about my business, emptying ashtrays and taking beer to people. I had to go out at some point, which meant going through the fire door because the club is on Times Square and when you go out you don't want to walk through 3,000 people to do so. So I get outside and Lenny Kravitz is outside the club, with his guitar, looking up like, 'How do I get in?' I ask him, 'Are you here to play with Prince?' 'How do you know 'bout that?' 'Well, I work here. Follow me, I'll take you up to Prince.' So I take out my key, open the door and take Lenny up the back stairs and down the corridor. I knock on the door again. There's the same soft 'Hello.' I open the door and Prince is standing pretty much in the same spot, hands in his pockets. He wasn't playing the guitar, or reading, he's just standing there. So I say, 'Hello, Prince. Lenny Kravitz is here to see you.' He's like, 'Lenny, Lenny, come on in,' and they start chatting. As I go to leave, Lenny turns round and says, 'That dude saved my ass. I couldn't get in the club.' Prince is like, 'Thanks, man, that's so cool.'

That was that. The one time I met Prince. He was a nice, cool dude and it's funny because, a lot of time, working in the service industries is a pretty good way to see what a person can be like. It's also funny to me that a lot of the times with these guys, it's always the people around them saying, 'Don't look at 'em, don't talk to 'em.' Generally, you meet these guys, and 98 per cent of the time they're pretty damn cool.

I really respect Prince. He's one of the guys who, to me, is a direct descendent of all the other greats I've talked about in this book, except Prince is the guy who learned from everybody's mistakes, studied them and didn't make them. The wildest shit Prince ever got into – apart from chasing women, maybe – was becoming a Jehovah's Witness. Ask people in Minneapolis if Prince ever turned up on the door, waving a copy of *The Watchtower*, and they'll tell you, 'Hell, yeah.' One time, the little guy turned up at this Jewish woman's house on Yom Kippur. She was like, 'Wrong crowd, Prince', but he still stayed for 25 minutes trying to spread the J-Love.

But otherwise, Prince has just concentrated on being pretty much the best musician walking the planet. He's been around since the Seventies, and this guy is still doing it five decades on – if anything, he just gets better and better. Prince cut his deal at 17 years old and he's 56 now. The dude's not ten years older than me and he makes me look like I didn't do shit! He's played music at its own game; whether just showing up on the day to do gigs like he did in London in 2014, or scribbling 'SLAVE' across his cheek when he began to feel stifled by Warner Bros, Prince has proven himself to be smart and sophisticated as well as an exemplary musician.

He saw what was going on. He was on the one both musically and intellectually. He made a movie with a soundtrack, *Purple Rain*, and when he put them out, it made him the biggest star in the world. He's also one of the best guitar players I've ever seen. He takes a lot of Hendrix and James Brown and that flashy Blues-man style like Buddy Guy, yet he's the unique derivative of all this great stuff. He's the last Rock star walking around that can enter a room and fuck it up. See him on piano, he kicks ass. Any instrument he plays – and he plays like 30 of them – he kicks ass. There's a song called 'Glass Cutter', which is a demo. He went in and played all the instruments and it's the illest riff. And it's just a demo. That's what he did just to mess around!

A guy like that learned the lessons that a lot of people didn't. He learned how to be on top of his shit; he knew every note of every band member playing at the same time. He's omnipotent on stage. He can do no wrong because he knows what's happening at all times. You can't fault what he does. The top YouTube video for 'Greatest Guitar Solo Ever' is from 2004 when they were inducting George Harrison into the Hall of Fame. Stevie Winwood, Tom Petty and Jeff Lynne are all playing – and at the end of this line up there's a guy in a red fedora, red shirt and black suit playing a Telecaster: Prince. He just destroys them all. At the end, he takes the guitar and throws it up in the air and walks away. The guitar doesn't come back down because he has his roadie up top to catch it. Prince is a cool motherfucker.

Like Hendrix and Jagger and Page, Prince has always surrounded himself with incredible players like Wendy & Lisa, Morris Day and Jam & Lewis. Prince's new band, 3RDEYEGIRL, are awesome too. I love them and I love that he has the three hottest chicks playing the shit out of Rock.

He's the amalgamation of all these things that make the greats so special: musician, composer, performer, writer, conductor. A lot of people sleep on Prince, but he's the most Rock dude out there. He put out the 3RDEYEGIRL record and his own on the same day. He gives his music out for free and then goes out and tours. He's really smart like that and he's been clever about his career. And he's never compromised any of his values. Who goes around Minneapolis knocking on doors with Larry Graham? Who does that? Prince. He does whatever the fuck he wants and people still appreciate him. He's written like, 500 hit songs or whatever, songs that we haven't even heard yet. He's prolific. He learned lessons. He's always on-point.

Prince is one of the last guys still doing it. You might not see him in the trash mags the whole time or performing at every big event, but he doesn't need to. He's just out there, selling his own music though his own label, playing great guitar and being awesome.

*

TEARS DRY ON THEIR OWN

Prince shows you don't have to self-destruct to be Rock 'n' Roll. And equally, self-destructive behaviour doesn't automatically equate to being Rock 'n' Roll: you need talent to back up attitude. If anyone was the portal between when you could get away with it and what you couldn't, it was Amy Winehouse.

Winehouse was the poster child for the new generation of Rock 'n' Roll because people almost forced her into it. They put so much pressure on her, and the press were portraying her as a car-crash celebrity. But Amy wasn't a celebrity; she was a musician. And, boy, did her music make you feel. She was an echo from a time gone by.

I did an interview with her one time. I was at the BRITs and Amy happened to walk by. She dropped her drink and shouted, 'Oh, my God, it's Huey!' I looked over and she's mouthing, 'I fucking love you.' Amy said, 'What are you doing here? I used to have a picture of you on my wall and, oh, the things I used to do to that picture.' Of course, she was high as a kite. I said, 'I'm here to do interviews with musicians', and she goes, 'You want to interview me?' She looked pretty high and pretty messed up, so I just stuck to asking her about music. She talked about Etta James and Bessie Smith and Billie Holiday and girl groups like The Supremes. She really knew her shit. I met somebody who, for most people, is the last remembrance of Rock 'n' Roll: drug-addled, tumultuous relationship, rehab, all that stuff that we associate with Rock 'n' Roll.

The thing I remember most about that interview with Amy was that she was very on-point. If you meet the highest person in the room and you touch on something that interests them the most, then somehow it's like they find this little space, this portal, that opens up and they talk to you really straight. I asked her, 'Who's your biggest critic?', and she said, 'Me! I'm not putting out anything with my name on it that sucks.' My mom watched it on YouTube and said, 'You were very nice to that girl.' And I was. I made a point to be. I'm not going to exploit her inebriation for the sake of a few extra views on YouTube.

They chased her to the grave, pretty much. It seemed that there was very little support around her. And her husband, who she should have been able to turn to, was a heroin addict. It just seems like everyone took advantage of Amy. It seemed that she felt that she was worthless, no matter what she did, which is sad. I could see when I met her that she was a tortured soul. You could also see that she was such a good person.

Amy put her heart and soul into it. It seems, ultimately, that it sucked the heart and soul out of her – and, eventually, the life too. We never got that third album from her. We can only guess at what she might be doing now if she had made it past 27. I think one thing is obvious, though; she'd be keeping it really, really real.

*

PAPA WAS A ROLLING STONE

For me, the truest definition of a living Rock 'n' Roll legend is Keith Richards. No one Rocked 'n' Rolled it like Keith and he is still there, still passionate about music, living and breathing it.

It's incredible to me that The Stones still tour together. With the Criminals, me and Fast have gone through our ups and downs as friends, but we're brothers because he's the only guy who knows what I've been through for the last 20 years. And vice versa. When you see Jagger drinking smoothies and going jogging in his tracksuit and then you see Keith with his headband and cigarette dangling from his mouth, it's so funny. But they still seem to get along great. I mean, 50 years in a band with someone? Marriages don't last that long. Lives don't last that long. The Stones was their life. And choosing to be a band in the first place says a lot. You're not thinking of going to the Royal Academy of Music to study Chopin. You're picking up a cheap Fender rip-off and you're trying to make the same three chords sound different to everybody else's three chords. And if by some chance you manage to get a hit record from it then suddenly all this money comes your way. Keith Richards is one of the good guys; I'm sure he's pissed a few people off along the way, but he gets my utmost respect because he remains a student of music. He really loves it and lives for it.

The Stones have never been able to fully shake off their posh-boy tag. After Nirvana, it felt like everybody in Seattle got signed, and the same thing happened with a lot of the bands in Britain after The Beatles. That's how The Stones got signed. They were like a connection to The Beatles but they were the new kids on the block, offering another kind of flavour. At first, they were written off as little more than a middle-class boy band. They lacked the working-class authenticity of Lennon and McCartney. But they put the work in and it turned out they were really talented dudes with a deep love and knowledge of the Blues. And what they didn't know, they set themselves to learning.

Keith is one in a billion. There are a lot of incredibly talented people, but Keith Richards was so perfectly in time and in tune with what was going on. He knew that it was the Blues that was doing it. And he's always paid homage. No matter how high he was, he was always on the one.

We're so obsessed with being inoffensive in society today that we've removed all the traits of rebels and renegades and Rock 'n' Rollers – being outlandish, spending your money, crashing things, breaking things, having rows in the street with your significant other, divorces, remarrying people half your age multiple times... Now artists have publicity managers and press advisors and damage-limitation experts; God forbid someone has sex with someone else or takes a toke on a joint.

We stopped walking on the wild side. People like Kurt Cobain, Jimmy Page and Jimi Hendrix constantly took risks. Can you imagine Keith Moon being allowed to run riot now, blowing up his drum kit on *The X Factor*? Smashing up a suite at Soho House? Passing out on stage because he was so wasted? Chucking cars and televisions into pools at the Holiday Inn? This is a guy considered to be one of the greatest drummers of our time – but if he was around now, we'd probably never get to see him because the manager would have him chucked out for losing every single one of the band's endorsements – second-greatest drummer of all time or not.

God forbid if Beyoncé acted like Nina Simone did back in the Seventies, raging about civil rights and rallying against the establishment. Imagine Katy Perry having had one too many wines before she got on stage and not quite hitting the high notes. She'd be torn to pieces. But back then we let stars like Simone live and let live, because she was providing the world with some of the most beautiful and innovative music we'd ever heard. And thank God she was raging and rallying – it's because of people like Nina Simone, and before her Billie Holiday, that musicians were key in the advancements of civil rights. Nowadays, you might get a celebrity chucking a bucket of icy water over themselves, but rare are the people who truly put their neck on the line and actively attempt to make a difference.

But there is hope out there – I see it flickering, and there's plenty of fuel around; we just need to reignite it. If, as a human race, we've already been able to produce these incredible musicians and this heart-wrenchingly beautiful, poignant, mind-blowing, Rockin' 'n' Rollin' music over the past 100 years, imagine what more we're capable of over the next century.

If you're really, really serious about doing music, then study the masters, consider what's gone before and create a new future. We need you. Music needs you.

*

PICTURE ACKNOWLEDGEMENTS

Plate Section 1

1 Pictorial Press Ltd/Alamy; 2 above Michael Ochs Archives/Getty Images;
2 below Fine Art Images/Heritage Image Partnership Ltd./Alamy; 3
Michael Ochs Archives/Getty Images; 4 above Mug Shot/ Alamy; 4 below
left Granamour Weems Collection/Alamy; 4 below right Tom Copi/Michael
Ochs Archives/Getty Images; 5 Moviestore Collection Ltd./Alamy; 6 above
left Granamour Weems Collection/Alamy; 6 above right Pictorial Press Ltd./
Alamy; 6 below Miles Davis, Birth of the Cool, Capitol Jazz, 1957; 7 Gilles
Petard/Redferns/Getty Images; 8 above Vernon Merritt III/Time & Life
Pictures/Getty Images; 8 below ITV/Rex Features.

Plate Section 2

1 Michael Ochs Archives/Getty Images; 2 below left INTERFOTO/Alamy;
2 above Pictorial Press Ltd./Alamy; 2 below right Fred W. McDarrah/Getty
Images; 3 Bob Gruen; 4 above right Pictorial Press Ltd./Alamy; 4 above left
UPP/Topfoto; 5 above INTERFOTO/Alamy; 5 below MARKA/Alamy; 6
Richard E. Aaron/Getty Images; 7 Mike Schnapp; 8 above right Grenville
Charles/Alamy; 8 below right Pictorial Press Ltd./Alamy; 8 below left Chi
Modu/Diverse Images/Corbis; 8 above left Michael Ochs Archives/Getty
Images.

*

PUBLISHER'S ACKNOWLEDGEMENTS

The Publisher would like to thank Sam Gregory, Josh Adley, Hattie Collins and Silvia Crompton for their involvement in the making of this book.